# PLEASE GIVE A DEVOTION —

## for All Occasions

# Please Give a Devotion for All Occasions

## Amy Bolding

BAKER BOOK HOUSE
Grand Rapids, Michigan 49506

This book is lovingly dedicated to my three sisters: Mrs. Jack Nyberg, Mrs. Paul Wheelus, Miss Nancy Ward, and my only brother John Ward.

# CONTENTS

JANUARY
1. Turn a New Page . . . . . . . . . . 9
2. Coats Off to the Future . . . . . . . . 13

FEBRUARY
3. The Winning Power of Love . . . . . . . 18
4. Early American . . . . . . . . . . . 23

MARCH
5. What Have We to Serve With? . . . . . . 27
6. March Winds and Sunshine . . . . . . . 32

APRIL
7. Easter Thoughts . . . . . . . . . . . 37
8. Joy from a Stone Rolled Away . . . . . . . 41

MAY
9. Mother's Day of Glory . . . . . . . . . 45
10. Is There a Mother in the House? . . . . . . 50
11. Memorial Day . . . . . . . . . . . 53

JUNE
12. God Gave Us Men . . . . . . . . . . 57
13. Luminous Lives—Graduation Glory . . . . . 61

JULY
14. Independence Day . . . . . . . . . . 66
15. Keep America Beautiful . . . . . . . . 70

AUGUST
16. Travel in Strange Places . . . . . . . . 73
17. Vacation for God or from God . . . . . . 77

SEPTEMBER
18. The Blessing of Work . . . . . . . . . 81
19. School Days for Young and Old . . . . . 85

OCTOBER
20. Discover New Lands . . . . . . . . . 88
21. Andrew the Discoverer of Men . . . . . 92

NOVEMBER
22. Thankfulness a Habit . . . . . . . . . 96
23. The Extra Blessings of Thanksgiving . . . . 100

DECEMBER
24. How Far to Your Bethlehem? . . . . . . 104
25. Christmas Lights . . . . . . . . . . 109

MISCELLANEOUS
26. Travel Stains (End of Year) . . . . . . 114
27. Stewardship . . . . . . . . . . . . 118

# 1

# Turn a New Page

*"... but this one thing I do, forgetting those things which are behind, and reaching forth unto those things which are before, I press toward the mark for the prize of the high calling of God in Christ Jesus."*

—*Philippians 3:13, 14*

We stand today on the threshold of a new year. What will we find when we turn the page? Will this new year mean the beginning of a new life for us? Will it be the beginning of a full voyage of three hundred and sixty-five days long? God will give us this year only once. When it is past it cannot be called back; the same time comes twice to none.

One Sunday night I passed clean sheets of drawing paper to six little children in my class. In the center of the table I placed a large box of crayons. Some of the children immediately began to draw pictures on their paper. One started to whine: "I do not know what to draw."

Another pleaded, "Please draw a kitty for me, I don't know how."

At the end of the activities period some of the children were very happy with what they had created. They were proud to have their names written on their work. Others had made a mess of their papers. One little child threw his paper in the waste basket.

We are God's children and today we stand facing a clean page. What will we do with it? What will it look like at the close of the year?

> 'Tis not what a man does that exalts him,
> But what a man would do.
>
> —Browning

As you look at this page so clean and fresh, be sure you do not mar it by looking back with regret at the year just passed. With Paul we must forget those things which are behind and press forward to new achievements.

I noticed in my class of five-year-old's, the ones who reached out first for the crayon and started to work, were the ones who seemed happiest with what they had accomplished.

Reach out quickly and start your New Year with enthusiasm, energy, and joy. Make a fresh new start; determine that this new page will not be marred with the same mistakes you made last year.

> Every day is a fresh beginning,
>   Listen, my soul, to the glad refrain,
> And in spite of old sorrow, and older sinning,
>   And troubles forcasted, and possible pain,
>   Take heart with the day, and begin again.
>
> —Susan Coolidge

What kind of a mark will you press forward to reach? Will it be the mark of the prize of the high calling of God in Christ Jesus. It costs something to be a Christian, to press toward the mark of the high calling.

This New Year will you pay the price by showing trust? You are helpless without God; so determine from the very beginning to trust in His power to keep you. He has kept you in the past; trust that He has a wonderful year in store for you.

Certain conditions are always imposed on the ones who would press forward to serve Christ. Christians must show self-restraint and a spirit of humility if they would feel divine guidance.

# TURN A NEW PAGE

We must not wrap our mistakes and offenses of the past around us. They must be forgotten in a determination to do better.

We are all called to serve with enthusiasm and devotion. But some are more zealous than others. Like children do when they run for a distant goal, some get ahead of the others. Some grow discouraged over world conditions—and what not—and stop trying. Remember, no matter how troubled the world, the Kingdom is still the Lord's and He is looking after it. "The earth is the Lord's, and the fullness thereof."

If we would write best for our Lord on this clean page of the New Year we must "sanctify ourselves." Joshua of old urged the people to sanctify themselves. We can accomplish this by being grateful for the way God has brought us thus far.

As you turn the page and put the Old Year out of sight, will you face the clean New Year not only with trust, self-restraint and humility, but with a spirit of obedience? You face a journey with a grand prize at the end. Be courageous and earnest, determined to succeed in your mission.

A small girl visiting her grandmother found a mother cat with four little kittens. "Oh, I wish I had four hands, so I could hold them all at one time," she cried.

"You must just choose one to keep, for one will keep your two hands busy," the grandmother told her.

Facing a New Year we think of so many things we want to accomplish, we wish we were several people. Yet like the little girl, we will do well to press toward the mark of the high calling with the talent we have.

May God give you a double portion of blessings as you determine to serve Him as best you can.

> Before the portals of the coming year,
>    I bowed my head and humbly then I prayed,
> "Oh Father, tell me how to walk with Thee;
>    The way is dark and I am sore afraid."

## PLEASE GIVE A DEVOTION—for All Occasions

Soon came the answer as I waited there,
   "The New Year is a gift from God above,
No matter what it gives you or withholds,
   You must trust God nor ever doubt His love."

"But when the burdens bend my spirit low,
   And sorrows come I cannot understand?"
Softly but surely came the voice I heard,
   "Then trust God more and tightly hold His hand."

"So many problems, Lord," I said at last,
   "So many ways to turn—how can I know
Which one is best?" I heard him softly say,
   "Hold thou my hand—I will not let you go."

Then suddenly my fears seemed small indeed,
   I felt a peace I never knew before,
The portals of the New Year opened wide,
   And God was waiting just inside the door.
                               —Selected

# 2

# Coats Off to the Future

*"Therefore if any man be in Christ, he is a new crea-*
*ture; old things are passed away; behold, all things are*
*become new."—II Corinthians 5:17*

Someone has said: "Hats off to the past; coats off to the
future."

We have traveled a circle of time and now are facing
another January—another beginning of the circle. The past is
past, and we salute it. Now we need to think about taking our
coats off to the future.

We are ready for another lap in the race of life. It is not
important for us to outrun those about us. We do not have to
push them aside for our own gains. But we must face our
future and decide what we will do with the life given us.

As we take our coats off to this future we need to plan a
strategy. For Christians that should be simple to plan. The
strategy of every Christian should be to serve God. We must
do as we are told in Isaiah 54:2: "Enlarge the place of thy
tent, and let them stretch forth the curtains of thine habita-
tions: spare not, lengthen thy cords, and strengthen thy
stakes."

Two little boys decided to spend the night in.the back
yard. They had a small tent to put up. After a lot of hard

work they crawled into the tent and settled down to go to sleep. The dog came nosing around and the tent fell down on the boys. They began to call for "daddy."

When the father came out to see what all the commotion was about, he found two little boys heaping abuse on the poor dog.

"Now boys, old Chip is not the one to blame," their father told them, "You need to drive the tent stakes down deeper."

With the father's help the tent was made secure and soon the two boys and the dog were sleeping soundly.

As the curtain of time rings down on the old year we have no way of knowing what the future will hold for us.

To live is to face problems. The world seems filled with more and more moral problems. The lists of problems is endless—with evil often in high places, with war and threats of war, with high prices. The Christian is not alone when he takes off his coat to fight the problems of life. The leader we follow has given us some wonderful weapons.

One of our great weapons is prayer. We have someone who likes to hear our prayers. We have a God who is willing and able to answer our prayers. With the Apostle Paul we can say, "I can do all things through Christ who strengtheneth me."

Another wonderful weapon, too often neglected, is Bible study. We must read the guide book if we are to know the Way.

We were once lost in New Mexico. Night was drawing near and we were running low on gasoline. We could see no place to stop for gas or lodging. When we thought we would have to give up in despair, a trading post loomed up in the distance.

"What happened to all the trading posts shown on the map?" we asked the attendant as he filled our gas tank.

"Oh, your map is old; this is a new road and so far mine is the only store moved."

The travel guide we have to study and follow will never

lead us wrong. It is a living word, and fits all times and all ages.

Then we face the New Year with a motive. We do not take our coats off to nothingness. We have a great goal, a wonderful motive, and an urgent mission—the bringing in of the Kingdom.

Does the mission, the motive, the urgency seem too great for the Christians to undertake? There is an answer for that problem. In Luke 10:2 we read, "Pray ye therefore the Lord of the harvest, that he would send forth laborers into his harvest."

We must win others to help us with this gigantic task. Unless we go to find them many will never be won; unless we go and tell them the good news many will never hear. So we have a great motive for taking off our coats to the future. We cannot tell everyone but we can tell those nearest us—in our daily work, in our town, in our pathway as we go about our responsibilities and pleasures.

So—let us cast off our coats to the future.

### A NEW YEAR RESOLVE

I will start afresh this New Year with a higher, fairer creed;
I will cease to stand complaining of my ruthless neighbor's greed;
I will cease to sit repining while my duty's call is clear;
I will waste no moment whining, and my heart shall know no fear.

I will look sometimes about me for the things that merit praise;
I will search for hidden beauties that elude the grumbler's gaze;
I will try to end contentment in the paths that I must tread;
I will cease to have resentment when another gets ahead.

I will not be swayed by envy when my rival's strength is shown;
I will not deny his merit, but I'll try to prove my own;
I will try to see the beauty spread before me, rain or shine;
I will cease to preach your duty and be more concerned with mine.

—Selected

Hats off to the past, it is past. Whether it was good or bad, it is past. Coats off to the future now before us. All people have some opportunities, make them count.

I heard of a man in prison who felt he had no way to make life worthwhile. One day working in the prison he found a footlength of hollow cane. He learned to play tunes by using his finger to cover and uncover the open end of the cane. One of the guards took a knife and made some holes along the cane. Soon the man was very popular with the other men because he could play songs. He used his opportunity; he found a bright side in darkness.

The New Year will go slowly if you let yourself be depressed and frustrated. Be busy, be happy, be useful and before you know it the circle will have been gone around again and a New Year will come.

### LIFE'S JOURNEY

Does the road wind up hill all the way?
  Yes to the very end.
Will the day's journey take the whole long day?
  From Morn to night, my friend.
                              —Christina G. Rosetti

As we enter a New Year our hearts should breath a prayer asking God to help us every day—to help us love those about us, for no one ever has too much love. Ask God to walk daily by our sides so close that others may see His likeness in us. We should ask God to make us gentle, kind and thoughtful—to make us so long to win others to Christ that we will seek to do some good every day.

We must not enter a New Year without being thankful for all the blessings of the past. We must be grateful for the peace in our hearts when the world seems in turmoil. We must thank Him for friends and freedom of worship.

We must dedicate our hands, our feet, our heart and mind to making this a year of service for our Lord.

I read a story about a lady in Indiana who owned a clock more than four hundred years old. The family records led her to believe the clock had not been stopped since 1803.

That clock no doubt is very precious to the owner. Yet we

# COATS OFF TO THE FUTURE

have hearts that will beat all our lives through without stopping. Are they useful?

### A WAY TO A HAPPY NEW YEAR

To leave the old with a burst of song,
To recall the right and forgive the wrong;
To forget the thing that binds you fast
To the vain regrets of the year that's past;
To have the strength to let go your hold
Of the not worth while of the days grown old,

### AND

To dare go forth with a purpose true,
To the unknown task of the year that's new;
To help your brother along the road
To do his work and lift his load;
To add your gift to the world's good cheer,
Is to have and to give a Happy New Year.

—Robert Beattie

# 3

# The Winning Power of Love

*"Keep yourselves in the love of God."—Jude 21*

*"We love him, because he first loved us."—I John 4:29*

*"For God so loved the world, that he gave his only begotten Son, that whosoever believeth in him should not perish but have everlasting life."—John 3:16*

How often we have heard the old statement, "You can catch more flies with honey than with vinegar."

Love is more powerful than hatred. We are often tempted in the heat of an angry moment to try winning a battle with angry words or ugly accusations. Everyone wants to be a winner. To be sure of being a winner we must teach ourselves to be a lover.

"A soft answer turneth away wrath: but grevious words stir up anger" (Proverbs 15:1).

We found a terrapin on the road one day. We put it in a sack and gave it to the children. They were very frustrated with the terrapin because he would not put his head out of the shell. When we reached home the children took him to the back yard. They placed him in a warm sunny place and in a few moments he put out his head and legs and started walking.

"He likes warm sunshine," they cried.

Don't we all draw up into a shell if we are abused? We like warm sunshine of love and kindness. So we must show simple, sincere kindness and love to those about us if we would win them for our friends and for our Christ.

It is only human to think of ourselves, our future, our success in life, our present well being.

We were visiting our daughter one Saturday. It was certainly the wrong day for a visit. The older girls were entering a contest at the school, the mother and father had an important engagement at the county seat and the rest of us were rushing around trying to get the foods, table clothes and such loaded for the girls' contest. The baby girl listened to us making the plans. The grandparents would take the girls to the school. The parents would dress up and go the other direction to their appointment. Suddenly she began to jump up and down and holler, "Who is going to keep me, who is going to keep me?"

With a quiet, sweet voice her mother replied, "You and the boys will stay down the road with the neighbors. They are very anxious for you to visit them."

The little one, not quite three, rushed to her room and began to try putting on her cap and coat.

Just one harsh word would have made her feel neglected and sent her into tears of self-pity. The kindness and love of her mother made her feel all planned-for and excited.

Do you sometimes wallow in self-pity and begin to cry; "Who will keep me, who will keep me?"

We forget for the moment that our Heavenly Father has already made plans for our future. He knows what we have need of even before we ask. He loves us.

Fanny Crosby, a well-known and well-loved hymn writer was famous among her friends for her happy attitude toward life. No one ever heard her sitting back complaining over the darkness of her days. A friend in England thought she knew the reason Miss Crosby could be so happy and brave, she wrote the following:

Sweet blind singer over the sea,
Tuneful and jubilant, how can it be
That the songs of gladness, which float so far,
As if they fell from the evening star,
Are the notes of one who never may see
"Visible music" of flower and tree?
How can she sing in the dark like this?
What is her fountain of light and bliss?
Her heart can see, her heart can see!
May well she sing so joyously!
For the King Himself in His tender grace
Hath shown her the brightness of His face.
—Frances Ridley Havergal

Many books and many stories have been written about people who made success of their lives in spite of hardships and handicaps. If you read these stories you will find the majority of people who succeeded had loving hearts. They were grateful for help and kindness, they were true friends to those who helped them.

If we would be winners we must work more and more to love the other fellow. All too often we are quick to condemn without knowing why people act as they do.

LOVE IS—

Slow to suspect—quick to trust
Slow to condemn—quick to justify
Slow to offend—quick to defend
Slow to expose—quick to shield
Slow to reprimand—quick to forbear
Slow to belittle—quick to appreciate
Slow to demand—quick to give
Slow to provoke—quick to conciliate
Slow to resent—quick to forgive
Slow to hinder—quick to help
For love's baptism—let us plead and pray!
—Selected

Historians rate the story of love behind the building of the Taj Mahal as one of the greatest romances of all history. A few years ago a group of men undertook to prove that the story was all wrong.

# THE WINNING POWER OF LOVE

We do not know positively about the story of the Taj Mahal, but we do know that the story of God's great love as told in John 3:16 is true. People through the ages have tried to tell us the Bible was untrue. They die and go to their eternal punishment. The Bible lives on. Love wins against the odds of scientists, scholars, skeptics.

A little girl sitting on the front steps of her home was singing the song, "Jesus Loves Me, This I Know." A neighbor who had no time for God heard the song and it reminded him of days long gone by when he was a small boy in Sunday School.

"How do you know Jesus loves you," he called to the child. "Have you seen him?"

"No Mr. King, I haven't seen him but I talk to him every night." The child went right on singing about Jesus.

Mr. King went into the house but the words kept ringing in his ears. A little cotton-haired boy came to haunt his memory. He tried to remember why that little boy had grown away from the love of Jesus. A few tragedies of his life came before him but they were past. He was well, he was successful but he was not happy. Suddenly he remembered the time when he had swallowed his penny at Sunday school. He began to laugh. How excited the teacher had grown. His mother, too, had been upset. All over a swallowed penny. He began to hum the tune. He went outside again and spoke to the child.

"Do you think Jesus loves an old man like me?"

"Oh, yes, Mr. King, he loves you but you should tell him you love him. You never go to church."

"I'll go next Sunday."

What power has love! Just as that man's life was changed and made happy because a little child reminded him of a love he had neglected, we can change lives with love.

"Keep yourself in the love of God" (Jude 21).

What a changed world we would live in if all people who name the name of Christ would keep themselves in love. If only they would live as though they really wanted to win the world with love.

### JEREMIAH 9:23

Let not the wise glory in wisdom;
  Let not the strong glory in might;
Let not the rich glory in riches,
  But let us all glory in right.

Let not the weak glory in weakness;
  Let not our eyes glory in sight;
Let not our tongues glory in talking.
  But let us all glory in right.

Let not our ears glory in hearing;
  Let not the tall glory in height;
Let not the brave glory in bravery.
  But let us all glory in right.

Let not the fast glory in swiftness;
  Let not the mind glory in light;
But let us all seek to serve Jesus,
  And let us all seek to do right.
  —J. T. Bolding

# 4

# Early American

*"These things have I written unto you that believe on the name of the Son of God; that ye may know that ye have eternal life, and that ye may believe on the name of the Son of God."—I John 5:13*

For a number of years we have been plagued by a rash of Early American stories. I love history and I love my country but I am persuaded many of the Western television shows are far from the real truth of early day happenings. One thing we can be sure of in all these stories, the hero is always going to win before the story ends.

John in the Scripture above wanted the followers of Christ to have perfect assurance of their salvation. We are saved by God's grace through faith. This excludes keeping a law, being moral, working hard in church. These are good but they do not save us.

Ephesians 2:8, 9 reads; "For by grace are ye saved through faith; and that not of yourselves; it is the gift of God: Not of works, lest any man should boast." Faith gives the glory of salvation to God in Christ Jesus.

Have you ever been closely associated with a so-called self-made man? When I was a child my father was pastor of a small country church. In that church we had one member who felt he was self-made. I never found out who unmade him for at that time he was poor except for a diamond ring he wore. No other man in our church wore a diamond ring so he attracted lots of attention.

One day while he was attending services he lost the diamond out of its mounting. The whole congregation was alerted to help search for his diamond. At last after much searching the stone was found and all turned to go home. One old lady was heard to say; "Sure good he found it because without that ring he could never make us believe the tales he tells about once being rich."

Like the heroes in the Westerns we have perfect assurance God has saved us. Before we are saved we are enemies of God. After conversion our lives are changed and when God sees us he sees Christ standing before our sins to blot them out.

"Therefore if any man be in Christ, he is a new creature: old things are passed away; behold all things are become new" (II Corinthians 5:17).

All people do not have the same experience of salvation but we all can have the assurances of God's love. All too often we depend on what we do or say to give us the assurance, as the old fellow who wore the diamond.

Salvation changes people's lives. The big change is from indifference to a longing to see others accept Christ. Love for others is a diamond all Christians should wear. "By this ye know that we have passed from death unto life because we love the brethren ... he that loveth not his brother abideth in death" (I John 3:14).

At times there are difficulties which hinder our assurance of salvation. We, at times, ask ourselves, "Have I repented enough?"

Repentance never could make a payment on your sins. Repentance is the change of attitude and mind toward God. If you have changed your heart and mind toward God it is because of repentance, yet Christ's blood saves us as we have faith in Him.

Because we are helpless humans Christ died for our sins,

24

that we might have a way of escape. Sometimes our human minds tell us that we must be saved by "feeling." Remember the poor thief on the cross. He looked at Jesus, suffering just as much as he was, and he recognized that Jesus was innocent.

"And he said unto Jesus, Lord, remember me when thou comest into thy kingdom." "And Jesus said unto him, Verily I say unto thee, Today shalt thou be with me in paradise" (Luke 23:42, 43).

The thief was dying. He had no way to work for Jesus; he had no gold to give to carry on Christ's Kingdom; yet Christ assured him of a home in paradise. Why? He acknowledged Him as Lord, and believed on Him.

It is only human to want assurance of love. Sweethearts send millions of valentines each year to assure each other of undying love. Do we find ourselves at times doubting God's love or our salvation, because some trial comes our way?

"And I give unto them eternal life; and they shall never perish, neither shall any man pluck them out of my hand" (John 10:28). This one verse is enough assurance for us that Christ will keep us safe in His love.

The evil spirit is always seeking to make people doubt; to make them useless Christians because of doubt. When we compromise with sin doubt comes in to destroy our peace of mind.

When God spoke to Noah he did not say, "Now here is a great ark, on the outside I have put some hooks you can hang onto, if you can cling to them for a certain number of days you will be saved from the flood. No! He told Noah and his family to enter into the ark. Then God himself closed the door and they were safe.

I have entered into the ark of salvation, God has closed the door. He will bring me safe to the harbor of Heaven. I am unworthy of such love, such salvation but Christ has blotted out all my unworthiness.

Hebrews 7:25, "Wherefore he is able also to save them to the uttermost that come unto God by him, seeing he ever liveth to make intercession for them."

I once knew a woman who did not believe her husband loved her. She would bore her friends with long stories of her doubts and concern. One lady grew so tired of hearing the tales over and over. One day when they started she roughly said: "Jill, if you would go home, clean the house from top to bottom, mend your husband's clothes and cook him a good supper, I bet he would show you he loved you."

Jill became angry, and left. I am glad to say that later she did show signs of improvement as a wife and her home became happier. You never hear Christians who are very busy working for the Lord complaining about the Lord not loving them.

### THE PRAYER OF LOVE

Dear Lord! Kind Lord!
  Gracious Lord! I pray
Thou wilt look on all I love,
  Tenderly today!
Weed their hearts of weariness;
  Scatter every care
Down a wake of angel-wings
  Winnowing the air.

Bring unto the sorrowing
  All release from pain;
Let the lips of laughter
  Overflow again;
And with all the needy
  O divide, I pray,
This vast measure of content
  That is mine today!
    —James Whitcomb Riley

# 5

# What Have We to Serve With?

*"I must work the works of him that sent me, while it is day: the night cometh, when no man can work."*
                                                              *—John 9:4*

*" ... To love the Lord your God, and to walk in all his ways, and to keep his commandments, and to cleave unto him, and to serve him with all your heart and with all your soul."—Joshua 22:5*

"I don't know what your destiny will be, but one thing I know: the only ones among you who will be really happy are those who will have sought and found how to serve," said Albert Schweitzer, the great man who gave his service for many years to the people of Africa.

In the early days of the state of Oklahoma my father was a missionary preacher. The churches were far apart and many times services were held one Sunday each month. That was a big Sunday and people planned to visit with each other after services. One woman always told her children to pause a moment on top of a high hill about a mile from their home. She had five children. If she counted more than five on top of the hill she knew the children were bringing home company. By the time the children and their friends had walked the last

27

mile she had killed another chicken and had it in the pan cooking. She never complained that it was her lot to stay home because she was not up to the long walk. On some occasions the team of horses would be hitched to the wagon, if they had not worked all week in the field, and she, too, could go to services.

Each family owned their own song book. The Sunday afternoons were spent singing the songs and talking. That pioneer mother set an example before her children of service to her family and friends. Often when the family and friends sat down to eat there would not be enough knives and forks to go around. The ones they had were usually bone-handle knives, silverware was rare in those new areas.

We live in an age when people have forgotten what it means to walk a few miles because they want or have to go somewhere. We do not have to watch the top of a high hill to get a message, we have telephones, radios, and television. With all our modern wealth and inventions we are still just as obligated to serve others as our forefathers.

There are many people today who would not open their front doors and help someone in need at that door. Yet those same people will cry for more "Foreign Aid." Are you sure a light that will not shine at your own door will light the way in a foreign land?

A story was carried nationwide about a poor boy walking home from work. Some boys, too lazy to work, robbed and beat him for the sum of sixteen cents. Badly hurt the boy knocked on seven doors begging for help before he found one who would call the police and an ambulance.

What do we have to serve with? How many years since you ate with a fork lacking one tine, or a knife with half the handle gone? W have so many things, we are forgetting that people are important. When Jesus said, "I must work the works of him who sent me. . . ," He was not thinking of making more money to buy more things. He was not thinking that the night of death would soon come and he could accumulate no more property to leave behind. He came to work for the souls of men. He came to make a way of salvation for all who would believe.

Christian people have more to serve with today than at any time in the history of the world. We are better educated, better informed. We can go from place to place easier. We do not have to work sixteen and eighteen hours a day to make a livelihood. Are we giving of ourselves? Are we sincerely giving our best selves or do we offer just a little token of worship once a week?

I heard a minister tell of the greatest prayer he ever heard prayed. A rough oilfield worker was converted during a revival. A few nights after his conversion the pastor called on him to pray. The audience sat spell bound, wondering what he could say to God. In the quiet of that agonizing moment they heard an anguished plea, "Oh Mr. Jesus!" and the man sat down sobbing like a child.

Why should we serve when others live for themselves? Our Lord commanded it: "Bear ye one another's burdens."

> For the soul that gives is the soul that lives;
> And bearing another's load
> Doth lighten your own, and shorten the way,
> And brighten the homeward road.
> —Selected

One of the nicest stories I have heard about bearing others' loads was told by a young ministerial student. One of the lady teachers in his school was planning to go on a lecture tour. She was very popular and beginning to be famous. The young man was asked to escort her from her office to the airport and see her safely aboard her plane.

All combed and dressed in his best he arrived at her office. She was ready and the time was a little short. As she was leaving the cleaning woman was arriving.

"How are you today, Bertha?" she asked, "I hope your husband is feeling better."

"Hurry, or we will miss the flight." the young man urged.

On the elevator at last the young man breathed a sigh of

relief. The teacher began talking to the girl operating the elevator. She asked her about her wedding plans and teased a little about her boy friend riding the elevator so much.

When the elevator stopped at one floor the oldest professor in the school stepped on. The woman took hold of his arm as if to steady herself but in reality to help him keep his balance better.

When they reached the ground floor the young man took her arm and would have hurried her out the door.

"I must tell the blind boy at the concession stand good-bye, he will miss me." She went to the stand and bought gum and candy.

At last they reached the airport just before the escort gave way to complete nervous jitters. When the teacher was safely on the plane the ministerial student sat a moment in his car and thought. Had she really taken so much time to make others feel loved and wanted?

No, not much, for she paused only a moment each time, yet, no doubt, all she spoke to would have a happier day because of her kindness.

As he sat there and relaxed a great lesson dawned on that young fellow who was planning to live the life of a minister. "I must always take time to be kind and help others."

The world is interested in popularity, power, position, fame and wealth. It wants to command, not serve. Jesus gave a new standard of greatness, in Mark 10:45, "For even the Son of man came not to be ministered unto, but to minister, and to give his life a ransom for many."

Jesus not only commands us to serve but he set the example of service himself. Selfless service constitutes a higher dignity for a man than any possible place of authority.

Many young ministers today have the false idea of their place. They feel the church is to serve them not they the church.

Jesus said to his disciples and I do not think the minister today has any later message, "But so shall it not be among you: but whosoever will be great among you, shall be your

# WHAT HAVE WE TO SERVE WITH?

minister: And whosoever of you will be the chiefest, shall be servant of all" (Mark 10:43, 44).

A news reporter visiting a mission hospital in a foreign land became ill with revulsion as he watched a nurse care for a very repulsive patient.

"There is not enough money in the bank to pay me to perform such a task," he told the nurse later.

"No nor me either," she smiled, "only love keeps me working. Christ called me to this work."

What have we to serve with?

## NOW

If you have hard work to do,
    Do it now.
Today the skies are clear and blue,
Tomorrow clouds may come in view
Yesterday is not for you;
    Do it now.

If you have a song to sing,
    Sing it now.
Let the notes of gladness ring
Clear as song of bird in spring,
Let every day some music bring;
    Sing it now.

If you have kind words to say,
    Say them now.
Tomorrow may not come your way
Do a kindness while you may
Loved ones will not always stay;
    Say them now.

If you have a smile to show
    Show it now.
Make hearts happy, roses grow,
Let the friends around you know
The love you have before you go,
    Show it now.

—Anonymous

# 6

# March Winds and Sunshine

*"The beloved of the Lord shall dwell in safety by him;
and the Lord shall cover him all the day long."*
                                    —*Deuteronomy 33:12*

*"The Lord is good unto them that wait for him, to
the soul that seeketh him."*—*Lamentations 3:25*

### SPRINKLE SUNSHINE

If you should see a fellow man with
    trouble's flag unfurled,
And lookin' like he didn't have a
    friend in all the world.
Go up and slap him on the back
    and holler, "How d'you do?"
And grasp his hand so warm he'll
    know he has a friend in you.
Then ax him what's a-hurtin him,
    and laugh his cares away,
And tell him that the darkest night
    is just before the day.
Don't talk in graveyard palaver, but say
    it right out loud,
That God will sprinkle sunshine in
    the trail of every cloud.

This world at best is but a hash of
    pleasure and of pain;

# MARCH WINDS AND SUNSHINE

> Some days are bright and sunny,
>   and some are slushed with rain;
> And that's just how it ought to be,
>   so when the clouds roll by
> We'll know just how to 'predicte
>   the bright and smiling sky.
> So learn to take it as it comes, and
>   don't swear if it pours,
> Because the Lord's opinion don't co-
>   incide with yours;
> But always keep remembering when
>   cares your path enshroud,
> That God has lots of sunshine to
>   spill behind the cloud.
>                    —James Whitcomb Riley

In West Texas we think of sand storms and March as going together. At times the sand blows so hard and thick cars must keep their head lights on and then they are not safe. The air overhead is often filled with flying objects which can break a windshield. On one such day not long back I was looking out the window when I saw a new trash barrel, lid on securely, go rolling down the side street. I knew that had to be my new container, although we have concrete holders for them. I looked at the barrel soon out of sight in the dust, and I thought about going after it. Going out into the storm seemed foolish, the sand cuts ones face and gets in eyes.

"The wind may be quieter by late this afternoon and we can go in the car to look for it," I promised myself.

When my husband came home at five-thirty the wind was blowing at a more reasonable gate. We got in the car and drove several blocks looking for our lost container. We came home empty-handed.

At times we as individuals feel our lives are in such turmoil from some kind of sorrow or misfortune. We stand and watch almost helplessly as it seems all we hold precious and dear is being swept away.

As my husband and I drove in the neighborhood looking for our lost property we saw a beautiful new house with a brick fence. The sandstorm had blown the brick fence over and crumpled it to pieces. Their trouble was worse and far more expensive than mine.

As we feel the sand storms and winds of life tossing us about we need to trust more fully in the one who makes the winds to blow, and who also makes the storm be still.

I could have gone out into the storm and rescued my property before it was completely gone, but I preferred waiting. We always know that perhaps the next day, or at most, the day after, will be beautiful and the sun will shine. Wouldn't it be wonderful if we as Christians could always remember when troubles surround us that God's love is just behind the cloud; that the sunshine of His love will shine more brightly after the storm.

"The Lord is good unto them that wait for him, to the soul that seeketh him" (Lamentations 3:25).

The house next door to us has a large, old apple tree in the yard. The limbs grow all the way to the ground and look as if the owner has never bothered to trim them. During the sandstorms when the tumbleweeds blow they stack up by that apple tree and reach almost as high as his house. Tumbleweeds are large round weeds growing on a single small stem. When the wind blows in the fall or spring the weeds snap off next to the ground and blow about. In new parts of the city the weeds have been known to blow and stack so high in people's doorways that the city fire department would have to take trucks and remove them.

Now isn't that old apple tree just like my life and yours? We let branches of worry, fret, envy and jealousy just grow and grow until all kinds of weeds catch on them and they stack so high as to become dangerous to our soul-health and happiness.

When I peep out the bathroom window and see the old tree I say; "I wish that man would trim his tree."

When our friends and relatives see us holding a grudge, nursing a grievance, or claiming a slight, I expect they say to themselves: "I wish she would get over being like that."

Sometimes we get attention for a little while because we

have problems. The lady who could not get out of her front door until the fire department removed the weeds, had her picture in the paper. But her house did not look pretty with all those weeds. Most of us gave a shrug and thought, "Glad it wasn't that bad at my house."

We may attract a little attention by being cross and sorry for ourselves, but is it worth it? Most everyone likes to be in the sunshine. We like people who have pleasant dispositions.

Storms will come to every life from time to time. The person who lives close to God each day will find that the sunshine comes back quicker. We do not always understand why storms come but we know who will lead us safely through to the sunlight.

As Christians we have an obligation and a duty to help those going through the storm clouds. We may think our word of comfort will not be appreciated or wanted but just the same let's give it.

A group of five friends were going hunting one morning. As the supplies were being passed out and loaded one man gave each of the others a small box of matches.

"I won't need these, I don't smoke." One of the fellows started to hand the box back.

"Keep it anyway for today, might meet someone who was out," his friend told him.

The men had walked and had fun most of the day but as night began to draw near they could not find where they had parked the pickup. They separated to look for it. Two of them soon realized they were lost.

"We could wander around in this thicket for days and not find the way out," they told each other.

The man who did not smoke felt in his pocket and brought out the matches. "I'll gather a few sticks and start a fire."

Soon the fire was going and their companions saw the glow of it against the sky. When all five were back together at the fire, they decided to keep the fire going and wait·for morning.

A cowboy saw the light several miles away and rode his horse out to see who had started a fire and was endangering the trees and grass.

After he found the men and led them back to their truck they began to thank the man who had started the fire.

"I had used all my matches," each one said in turn.

God gives all of his children some abilities for helping others. We may think we will never need them but at the least expected time a word from us may help clear away the storm and bring the sunshine.

"How beautiful upon the mountains are the feet of him that bringeth good tidings" (Isaiah 52:7).

I wiped a tear from off my brother's face,
And suddenly God spoke, and gently smiled,
  "Thank you, my child,
Someday I'll wipe the tears from every face;
Till then, you take my place!"

Now since that day, these hands of mine are His,
Who formed the world, the stars, and all that is.
My hands, so frail, and weak, O wonder grand!
Are deputy for God's almighty hand.
         —Annie A. Ziedman

### CONSTANT FRETTING

What's the use of constant fretting?
  Christ the Lord is very nigh,
Let us not, his love forgetting,
  Turn our song into a sigh.

God's bestowed on us his blessing,
  So abundant and so free,
And he never leaves us guessing,
  For his love in Christ we see.
         —J. T. Bolding

7

# Easter Thoughts

*"If ye then be risen with Christ, seek those things which
are above, where Christ sitteth on the right hand of God.
Set your affection on things above, not on things on
the earth"—Colossians 3:1, 2*

### CHRIST IN GETHSEMANE

It makes my heart rejoice to know,
    An angel came from up above,
To the garden of Gethsemane,
    To bless the Lord with Heaven's love.

There Jesus knelt and prayed alone,
    While friends slept near an olive tree.
There He agreed to take the cross;
    To give His life for you and me.

I know Peter, James, and John,
    Had not the slightest thought that night,
Of things that soon would come to pass,
    To bring them sorrow, anguish, fright.

But when I think of Christ alone—
    In Garden of Gethsemane;
I'm sorry someone wasn't there,
    To watch with Him for you and me.

I'm glad an angel came to Him,
And Heaven's light upon Him shone,
While Jesus consecrated all,
That for our sins He might atone.
—F. M. Bates

The first Easter sermon ever preached can be found in the Revised Version John 20:18, "I have seen the Lord." This sermon was preached by Mary Magdala, one who had been looked upon with contempt, pity and distrust.

Perhaps Mary did not realize the full meaning of her message, "I have seen the Lord." A message that would change the life and thinking of all who heard and believed.

Mary had gone to the tomb to perform a service. She went to the tomb with a broken heart and left the tomb with a message, a message that was to live and change people as long as time shall be. "I have seen the Lord."

We do not understand all about the resurrection but it is enough to know He lives. It is enough to know death has been conquered, the power of the grave has been broken.

When I was quite a young woman I went with my husband to the home of a church member whose husband had died very suddenly. She kept saying over and over, "Death is so final, death is so final."

I Peter 1:3 reads, "Blessed be the God and Father of our Lord Jesus Christ, which according to his abundant mercy hath begotten us again to a lively hope by the resurrection of Jesus Christ from the dead."

A person who has really seen the Lord will know that death for a Christian is just the stepping into a better place; a going to sit with Christ in Heavenly places.

Christ won for his followers the battle against death. His resurrection meant the overthrow of death. Many men have given their lives for the promotion of the gospel. Christ's resurrection proved that God had accepted and approved of the work of redemption wrought by Christ.

"If ye then be risen with Christ, seek those things which are above."

# EASTER THOUGHTS

Jesus prophesied that he would rise again. Followers saw him and talked with him after the crucifixion and burial. The disciples were so sure of life eternal they were willing to proclaim the death, burial and resurrection of Christ even if it meant an early martyrdom for them.

The world-wide effects of the belief in his resurrection has caused Christianity to flourish in the face of all persecutions.

Many years have passed since I had to stand with a broken heart and hear the woman cry, "Death is so final." Since that time I have grown wiser and older and known loss myself. Many times have I heard a good Christian whisper in anguish, "I'll meet you soon over there," and then go out to live for God and Christ's kingdom until the time for that meeting came.

No, death is not a final parting for those who are trusting in Christ, those who have been buried to their old sins and have arisen to walk anew with Him.

Have you ever wondered why Christ did not wait to come to earth until we had radio and television and telephones. Why the message could have been flashed around the world in a few moments. Why come first to a woman who had been so wicked before she met Christ? Why have one poor redeemed sinner run and say, "I have seen the Lord?"

Today the only way people will be turned from their wicked ways is by hearing someone say, "I have seen the Lord."

We as Christ's followers have a personal message to give. Only as we give it will the world turn to Christ. Are we risen with Christ?

### THIS BODY IS MY HOUSE

"This body is my house—it is not I;
Herein I sojourn till, in some far sky,
I lease a fairer dwelling, built to last
Till all the carpentry of time is past
When from my high place viewing this lone star,
What shall I care where these poor timbers are?

## PLEASE GIVE A DEVOTION—for All Occasions

The ancient heavens will roll aside for me
As Moses monarched the dividing sea.
This body is my house—it is not I.
Triumphant in this faith I live and die."
—Frederick Lawrence Knowles

# 8

# Joy from a Stone Rolled Away

*"And they said among themselves, Who shall roll us away the stone from the door of the sepulchre? And when they looked, they saw that the stone was rolled away: for it was very great."—Mark 16:3, 4*

### EASTER

My risen Lord, I feel thy strong protection;
I see thee stand among the graves today;
I am the Day, the Life, the Resurrection,
  I hear thee say,
And all the burdens I have carried sadly
Grow light as blossoms on an April day;
My cross becomes a staff, I journey gladly
  This Easter day.

—Author Unknown

During my years of growing up I often heard friends tell of a wonderful trip they made at Easter. They went to Lawton, Oklahoma to see the Easter story acted out by people who spent time and money to produce the great pageant. The pageant took place in an open air theatre.

People would take food and blankets in order to spend the night and be in a good position to hear and see on Easter morning. Oh how I longed to make that trip to Lawton. I felt that I could almost see Jesus step forth from the tomb as I heard glowing reports of the pageant.

The followers of Jesus did not wait at the tomb, they did not expect a great event to happen. They had been told that he would be back in three days. They failed to believe and understand. They were lost in their own despair and sorrow.

As the women went toward the tomb that morning their minds were filled with the problems they faced. They thought of the great heavy stone in front of the opening. How could they move such a stone. Who would move it for them?

They were typical people. We go along looking at our problems, the ones we have and the ones we expect to find, failing to realize God already has solved them.

Mary found the tomb to be, not a place of death but a place of life, not of despair but of hope.

Mary found the tomb to be a place where she found comfort, "Be not afraid!" She found it to be a place of hope because the stone was rolled away and the resurrection of Christ a fact, not a promise.

Because He lives we shall live also!

### SINCE CHRIST AROSE

Since Christ arose
The grave has lost its terror;
We know that death no longer can dispose
Of life, which is not fleeting, but eternal,
Unlocking heaven's gate—
Since Christ arose.

Since Christ arose
He is the mighty victor,
Dispelling doubt and crushing earthly foes,
And thus to all is offered full salvation,
And strength for every task—
Since Christ arose.

—George Wiseman

At the tomb Mary found new power and new zeal for a world wide task. She started by telling those she knew best.

# JOY FROM A STONE ROLLED AWAY

We must start to roll away the stone which hides our Saviour from the world by telling others what we saw when we gave our own hearts to Christ. We must tell how we felt when his love came in to fill our lives with hope and glory. We must roll away the stone by telling what we have heard as Jesus calls to us each day. Most of all we must show the change in our own lives by the way we live each day.

In a small town all the churches would meet early Easter morning in the park. There, Christians would sing and pray and testify, closing the service with a sermon by a local pastor.

Two boys about half-grown were there one Easter morning, not because they wanted to be, but because their parents brought them.

"I hope you can prove to us we didn't loose our sleep for nothing," one of the boys told his pastor before the services started.

"Oh yes, I can easily do that," the pastor assured him. "You listen closely and I will bring out my proof before the sermon ends."

The boys went to one side and sat down to listen and scoff. The services were not long. Most of the people were there to worship and the spirit of God could be felt.

Suddenly in the middle of his sermon the pastor stopped. "Look," he pointed to the rays of sunshine just beginning to come up in the east.

As all the people looked and enjoyed the beauty of the rising sun, he looked at the two boys. "The world was once lost in darkness, as dark as last night, but the Son of God came forth from a tomb and brought the glory of sunshine to the world. All about us we can see the little flowers coming up to grow and make the world more beautiful. All things and people have their time to live on this earth, then they too must be gone for awhile. Mothers and fathers give their lives working for their children, then they go to their eternal home leaving the children to carry on.

"If Christ had not come forth from that tomb we would indeed live hopeless lives but we live in hope of a great resurrection day."

The park with its early spring leaves and a few tulips blooming in the beds had never looked so beautiful. The people started for home as the last notes of "Up From the Grave He Arose," died away.

The two boys went along eager for a hot breakfast and freedom to laugh and talk, but with them went the secure joy of knowing there was a life after death to look forward to.

Jesus talked of his coming death to the disciples but he also talked of the coming resurrection. They go together.

# 9

# Mother's Day of Glory

*"For this child I prayed; and the Lord hath given me
my petition which I asked of him. Therefore also I have
lent him to the Lord, as long as he liveth he shall be lent
to the Lord."—I Samuel 1:27, 28*

The hearts of Americans were touched by a story in the
newspapers last year. The story was not about some great
hero or scientist. The story was of a mother, far from home,
crying out, "I must see my sons before I die." This mother
just thirty-seven years old had come to America from Mexico
in order to be treated for cancer. For three years she did not
see her two sons. Each day her heart cried out, "I must see my
sons before I die."

Some kind reporter wrote the story in a California paper
and in just a few days kindhearted people sent in enough
money to bring the two boys and their grandmother to the
bedside of the dying mother. Kindhearted nurses in the hospital bought Christmas gifts for the boys to give them in their
mother's room.

What a happy reunion that was. Three years makes lots of
difference in the growth of two boys but to that mother they
were still her precious little ones.

Hannah had longed so much for a child. When God answered her prayer she was willing that the child should serve God in the temple. What a sacrifice for Hannah! She had faith and hope that her son would be a great blessing to his people.

The most beautiful thing in the world today is the life of a pure, sweet, unselfish mother. Hannah was an example of a praying mother. Fortunate indeed are the children who have praying mothers.

### A MOTHER'S PRAYER

Father in Heaven, make me wise
So that my gaze may never meet
A question in my children's eye.
God keep me always kind and sweet.

And patient, too, before their need;
Let each vexation know its place,
Let gentleness be all my creed,
Let laughter live upon my face.

A mother's day is very long,
There are so many things to do!
But never let me lose my songs
Before the hardest day is through.
—Margaret E. Sangster

No one has ever been born into the world without a mother. Someone has beautifully said; "God couldn't be everywhere and so He made mothers."

I think Christian mothers would say, "I could not be a successful mother unless God was always at my side helping solve the problems of everyday."

Some children lose their mothers at birth, some lose them while they are young. Fortunate indeed are the children who have mothers until they are adults. Extra fortunate are children who have mothers who walk daily with God and talk with him.

From years of observation an educator told me the well-adjusted children in his school were the ones who ran home

after school and entered the door calling, "Mom, I'm home!"
And mom was always there to answer the call. No amount of
money or worldly success can take the place of the security a
child feels when they know "Mom" is there.

My mother is old and lives alone. I am old and do not get
to visit her often but I notice when I go to the door I always
call out, "Mother, it's me."

### MOTHER'S DAY

Every day is mother's day
  Tempting, puzzling, dear,
Bumps to kiss and cuts to bind,
  And sorry hearts to cheer;
Willful ways to coax aright,
  And laggard souls to hurry
Holes to patch and meals to plan,
  And lots of chance to worry.

But troubles bloom to wisdom,
  Patience grows to power,
And love, that was the reason,
  Is the wage for each crammed hour.
And every day that mothers make
  Diligent and sweet,
Speeds the time till that great day
  When hope and harvest meet.

—Selected

Too many mothers today are trying to buy happiness for
their children in stores. True happiness for children can only
be bought by love, service and sacrifice. Happy homes are the
ones where love is practiced and lived each day in the home.
A mother once had the habit of saying to her children,
"Things are never as black as they are painted, so long as we
have each other."

Looking back at Hannah the great mother who lent her
son to the Lord, we can learn some lessons.

First of all, she had love for God in her heart. She loved so
much she was willing to let God have her greatest treasure.

Second, Hannah had influence. Her child respected her

47

judgment and was willing to go and live in the temple. Samuel's first ideas about God came from his mother.

Thomas A. Edison spoke of his mother, "My mother was the making of me. She was so true. She was so sure of me; and I felt I had someone to live for; someone I must not disappoint."

Third, Hannah was a mother who would sacrifice. She showed unselfish devotion. There are many stories of selfish mothers filling our papers today. There are mothers who will starve or beat their children because they are in the way of their pleasure. The papers forget to publish the multiplied thousands of stories of quiet gentle mothers who make sacrifices for their children.

I have a friend who sends her son to a camp in the mountains each summer for a month. She is a widow and the camp is quite expensive.

"Why do you send him?" I asked, "He could work and help on his school clothes, the time he spends there."

"I send him because I grew up in the country and the thoughts of the beautiful woods and open country still lives in my heart." She brushed back her greying hair. "He will see the glories of God's world in the mountains."

Once I was invited over to see the pictures the boy took at the camp. His mother lived each moment over with him as he told about the animals, the trees, the other boys. I hope that boy when he is grown and, I hope successful, will send his mother for a vacation. She so willingly does without rest now that he may have a change.

Hannah planted courage in the heart of her son. How much we need mothers of courage today. Mothers fight a battle against the evil forces which would engulf their children each day. It takes courage to say "no" when most of the others are saying "yes."

Then last of all, mothers must be an inspiration to their children. A mother is functioning in her highest sphere when she is inspiring her children to reach for the best in education and service to the world.

# MOTHER'S DAY OF GLORY

## MY ALTAR

I have listened to God in His temple,
I've caught His voice in the crowd,
I have heard Him speak where the breakers
Were booming long and loud;
When the winds played soft in the treetops
My Father has talked to me,
But I never heard Him clearer
Than I did at my Mother's knee.

—Selected

# 10

# Is There a Mother in the House?
## (Christian Home Message)

*"Forsake not the law of thy mother."—Proverbs 6:20*

*"The eye that mocketh at his father, and despiseth to obey his mother, the ravens of the valley shall pick it out, and the young eagles shall eat it."—Proverbs 30:17*

Someone has very aptly said, "Home is the father's kingdom, the mother's world, and the child's paradise."

When we cannot say the above about our homes then we should take stock and seek to make them better. Every child deserves a Christian home. A Christian home is a home where love for each other is placed above love for self, and love for God is placed above all others.

A Christian home is built upon a strong belief in God—a belief that will stay firm in the face of trouble and adversity. A Christian home is one where the word of God is read, consulted and discussed.

I grew up in a home where we were taught that God would always work out our problems. We had a usual time for family prayers but there would come times when some emergency would swamp us and then we knew what would happen.

## IS THERE A MOTHER IN THE HOUSE?

"Let us all come into the living room for a word of prayer," my dad would say.

After he read a few promises from God's word the whole family would kneel in prayer. Sometimes daddy prayed a long time, then he called on mother to pray. When we left that room, as far as I was concerned, God was in charge and the problem would be solved in His own time.

Another great foundation stone for the Christian home is respect. Respect for the mother and father as well as respect for the children. I knew a little girl who felt her mother was not quite as patient with the family cat as she should be. One day she was exasperated when her mother told her not to feed the cat in the house.

"Mommie please don't blame Tabby. She thinks she is a people."

Children should be taught that their mother is someone who went down into the valley of the shadow of death in order to give them life, that they should respect and honor her. They should be made to realize that the father in the home often grows tired and weary from working but he considers it a duty and a privilege to support his family.

Blessed are the parents who can make home so attractive for their children they will not be constantly seeking entertainment elsewhere.

When I was growing up there was no money for fancy games but I have played many happy games of checkers on a checker board drawn off on the top of an apple box. We used white buttons and colored buttons for the checkers. Now, as far as I can remember, I never really felt deprived.

Far too often parents fail to ask with whom their children are spending their time. When they have been led into trouble by the wrong companions it is too late to inquire about their friends.

Home should be a place where we are as polite to our loved ones as we are to strangers away from home. The time to stop children from bickering is when they are first old enough to demand their way from another child. Something that is never allowed to start is not hard to stop.

In Proverbs 15:17 we read; "Better is a dinner of herbs where love is, than a stalled ox and hatred therewith."

In other words many a poor man goes to his home with a happier heart than many rich men. We must develop a sense of values.

A man was visiting our town one time and speaking in our church. One of the young men in the church asked the speaker to go home with him. Later he told my husband, "I didn't like that speaker's sense of values."

Do we practice at home what we preach away from home?

The peace that is the sweetest isn't born of minted gold,
And the joy that lasts the longest and still lingers when we're old
Is no dim and distant pleasure—it is not tomorrow's prize,
It is not the end of toiling, or the rainbow of our sighs.
It is every day within us—all the rest is hippodrome—
And the soul that is the gladdest is the soul that builds a home.
For the only happy toilers under earth's majestic dome
Are the ones who find their glories in the little spot called home.

—Selected

# 11

# Memorial Day

*"And Moses said unto the children of Israel, Remember this day."—Exodus 8:3*

*"Come behold the works of the Lord . . . he maketh wars to cease unto the end of the earth; he breaketh the bow, and cutteth the spear in sunder; he burneth the chariot in the fire. Be still and know that I am God: I will be exalted among the heathen, I will be exalted in the earth."—Psalm 46:9, 10*

### THEY DO NOT DIE

They do not die who leave their thought
    Imprinted on some deathless page,
Themselves may pass; the spell they wrought
    Endured on earth from age to age.
And thou, whose voice but yesterday
    Fell upon charmed listening ears,
    Thou shalt not know the touch of years;
Thou holdest time and chance at bay.
    Thou livest in thy living word
    As when its cadence first was heard.
                —T. B. Aldrich

Do you know someone whose existence is as meaningless and colorless as a clam. The most effective lives are not like that. They are full of sharp struggles, they make life eventful with conflicts. So I would remind you that the lives of the ones we remember on Memorial Day are those who gave their lives in struggle for something.

Memorial Day was first a day set apart by the Northern States for decorating the graves of the soldiers of the Union army. On May 5, 1868, General John A. Logan appointed May 30 as a Memorial Day. This date is a legal holiday in the United States and is thought of as the day we honor our war dead.

We seek God's presence as we pay tribute to our war dead who died in the service of their country that we might have the great nation we enjoy today.

Is war just something you read about in the morning paper?

During World War II, I lived near a family who became rich off the increase in property values. They had no sons to go to war. "I guess the government will take all we have and give it to the soldiers and their wives," the mother of the home would say spitefully.

I happened to be one of the wives who had not seen her husband for many months. My allotment was small compared to the profit that woman had made yet she was mean and spiteful. Sometimes I wished she could suffer just enough to make her appreciate what men were doing. Two houses away from her a family lost their only son in battle but she did not even bother to go and say a kind word. Flowers find a sweet use when they shed fragrance on a soldier's grave. We can always say kind words for the sacrifice they have made. Ours is a big debt, we will not be apt to overpay it.

Many men who fought and died on foreign battle fields did not fight for themselves but for the loved ones they left safe at home. They killed that our country might be free.

The purpose of Memorial Day should be twofold. There should surely be flowers and speeches for the dead, in sacred memory, but there must also be exhortations for the ones left at home and still living.

# MEMORIAL DAY

### AWARE

Help me, dear Lord, to be aware
Of what you've done for me;
Of all your providential care
And what you'd have me be.

May I not ask what I'm to get
From morning until night,
But live each day without regret
And in your will delight.

My hands, my feet, my all I give,
Dear Lord for service true,
And pray that you will help me live
For Christ in all I do.

O Lord, your ways I want to go,
In peaceful days and strife;
Please help me seek thy will to know,
And live a Christ-like life.
                         —J. T. Bolding

The greatest peril of our land is the decay of heroic manhood. Too many people are marching for the wrong causes, we need more fighting for the enforcement of law and order. The greatest tribute we can pay to those who gave their lives in the service of our country is to promote and obey the civil laws of our land.

The great ingredient that is lacking so much now is the will to be self-sacrificing. We want all for us and nothing for others.

If we anchor our hearts and souls in Christ, we may have loved and lost for a little while but we can be confident of seeing them again.

Jesus was the greatest example of self-sacrifice of all times. We should learn to imitate him more and more.

We, the living, must dedicate ourselves to the tasks that remain to be accomplished. Each year Memorial Day is a solomn reminder of what a costly thing war is. It cost lives of our young men, separation of families, destruction of property. It makes heavy burdens of debt and taxation on our country.

### NAMELESS MEN

Around me, when I wake or sleep,
Men strange to me their vigils keep;
And some were boys but yesterday
Upon the village green at play.
Their faces I shall never know;
Like sentinels they come and go.
In grateful love I bend the knee
For nameless men who died for me.

There is no earth or heaven or room
Where I may flee this dreadful doom.
Forever it is understood
I am a man redeemed by blood.
I must walk softly all my days
Down my redeemed and solemn ways.
Christ, take the men I bring to Thee,
The men who watch and die for me.
　　　　　　　　　　—Edward Shillito

We must put on the armor of righteousness as given in God's word (Ephesians 6:11, 13). Wear that armor proudly for we fight in a war that will never end until Christ comes again.

# 12

# God Gave Us Men

*"The rich and poor meet together: the Lord is the maker of them all."—Proverbs 22:2*

*"So God created man in his own image, in the image of God created he him."—Genesis 1:27*

In the animal kingdom the parents soon forget their children and push them out to make their own way in the forest. In the human world we hold our families very dear. We are not isolated individuals, mating, bringing children into the world, going away and leaving them to live as best they can.

God made man in his own image; therefore man is very special. We would be most miserable if we thought God for one hour was going to forget us, was going to go away into the forest of life where we could not reach Him or call upon Him. God needed man for communion with himself and God made man in such a way that man needs man.

So very much today our world needs to awake to the importance of the family and family life. God gave us men for a special purpose. Men to be the fathers of the human race, men to be the breadwinners of the world, men to fight dangers and to uphold truths.

On Father's Day we like to think of our own fathers and the happiness they brought to our lives. Men have a peculiar responsibility in life. God made some with the ability to paint, some to write, some to build, some to till the soil. Every talent you can name, except one, God has given to some men. The one left out is the ability to be a mother.

If we have been blessed with a wonderful Christian, earthly father, then we have a little taste on earth of what our heavenly father is like.

Jesus taught us to look upon God as our Heavenly Father, ever ready to hear our prayers and petitions.

God gave us men, men to make the world a better place. Men owe a duty to their children in three ways: Spiritual, mental, and physical. These three phases of a child's life can be influenced by others but the father is man of the house and he is directly responsible.

One Sunday a little girl asked her daddy to go to Sunday School and church with her. He said he was too tired, although he had played eighteen holes of golf the day before.

The little girl and her mother went alone to the services. At a stop light on the way home the car was hit broadside and the child was killed. The father's grief was very great. He suffered from guilt as well as loss. "If I had been driving," he kept repeating. Whether a father likes the present pastor or not he has a spiritual privilege to go with his family to the Sunday services.

Many men forget that they have a responsibility to their children mentally. They should see that the children attend school, that they have the things that are necessary for their comfort and well-being in school.

It doesn't hurt children to be careful with pencils and paper, to take care of jackets and mittens. What causes the trouble is the fact that so many parents do not take the trouble to explain to children why it is best not to be wasteful with school supplies.

The first school in which I taught, many years ago, a little, first grader asked his dad for a penny (can you believe the price) to buy a new pencil the second day of school.

"But, son, I gave you a new pencil to start school with yesterday!" The father exclaimed.

"I know you did daddy but they have a grinder up there."

The little fellow learned the hard way that grinders were to be used in times of need, not just for fun.

A father has a responsibility to teach his children how to have good, strong bodies. He has a duty to take them to doctors when they need help.

God gave us men to train us to share, to pray, to live in love and peace together, to make the world a better, happier place.

God gave us men to teach by example and by precept.

Last spring my husband had an apricot tree all tied up and staked out. "Those ropes look horrid," I complained.

"The tree is growing crooked and I want it straight," he replied. "You will be proud of it when I take the ropes away."

So God gave us fathers to teach and train and punish if necessary, in order to make the children grow fine and good.

A good father is always a knight in shining armor to his children. Their love and respect should be worth more than all the pleasures for a moment of bad company or of fame and fortune which takes a father's time completely away from his children.

### THOUGHTLESSNESS

A little bit of hatred
 can spoil a score of years
And blur the eyes, that ought to smile,
 with many needless tears.
A little bit of thoughtlessness
 and anger for a day,
Can rob a home of all it's joy
 and drive happiness away.

# PLEASE GIVE A DEVOTION—for All Occasions

A little bit of shouting,
  in a sharp and vicious tone,
Can leave a sting that will be felt,
  when many years have flown.
Just one hasty minute of uncontrolled
  ill temper can offend,
And leave an inner injury
  that years may never mend.

It takes no moral fibre,
  to say harsh and bitter things,
It doesn't call for courage
  to employ a lash that stings.
For cruel words and bitter
  any fool can think to say,
But the hurt they leave behind them,
  many years can't wipe away.

Just a little bit of hatred
  robs a home of all delight,
And leaves a winding trail of wrong
  that time may never right.
For only those are happy,
  and keep their peace of mind,
Who guard themselves from hatreds,
  and words that are unkind.

                    —Author Inknown

# 13

# Luminous Lives—
# Graduation Glory

*"And Moses was with the Lord forty days and forty nights,...and Moses' face shone while he talked with him."—Exodus 34:28, 29*

### YOUR NICHE

There's a niche for you in the world, my boy,
A corner for you to fill;
And it waits today along life's way
For the boy with a frank "I will."
So, lad, be true; the world wants you
In the corner that you may fill.

There's a niche in the world for you, my girl,
A corner for you to fill;
And a work to do which no one but you
In God's great plan can fill.
So, dear, be true, the world wants you,
And your place is waiting still.

—Selected

Have you ever been to a party, having a good time, when someone walked in the door and all the atmosphere seemed changed? Some people are so full of life, so radiant that they change the feelings of all around them. Then there are people who make others want to just walk away when they come near. They always have slighting remarks to make or ugly comments. Of course, the great majority of people are just one of a crowd, not many pay them any attention. They are missed very little when they are absent.

As graduates you are about to go out into the world. What type of impression do you plan to make? Will you strive to be popular, successful, famous, or nothing?

It is possible for every young person to live a luminous life. A life so glowing that others want to be in your presence. Others want to be your friend. We can take our cue from Moses.

Moses had been with God. He had spent forty days and forty nights on a mountain in communion with God. You are about to enter into the world of business, marriage, sports, competition for daily bread. You, too, should take time to commune with God about the future you face.

Communion with God will show in your daily life, being with God will give your face a glow most people do not have. Thinking about God will help make you make right decisions when you are faced with choices.

"I pray each day," you might say, "Yet I can't say that I have a luminous life."

When Moses took time to commune with God he gained a knowledge of God. From this knowledge he became the great writer and law-giver of the first books in the Bible. All of you have attained in scholastic knowledge. You must now leave mother's and father's protecting wings and go out into the throngs of people to make your own place.

From the knowledge Moses gained came inspiring visions of things he must do with the people he led. If you with your knowledge of books have not gained visions of what there is to do in the world you of all people need to stop and commune with God.

If your heart is filled with visions of what you want to accomplish, then those visions will help keep you pure. Do not let a foolish moment of temptation take all the glow from your life.

# LUMINOUS LIVES—GRADUATION GLORY

In a small High School a young man was president of the student body. He was a star on the football team. He sang in the church choir on Sunday. Then he started going with a girl who had only the wrong kind of visions in her pretty head. Suddenly the young man's world crashed about him. The visions of his future had failed to keep him pure. He was forced to marry before he could finish his senior year. He had to drop out of the football team, he had to resign as president of the student body.

One of the teachers in the school had tried to keep her pupils from such pitfalls. They had laughed in her face and called her old fashioned. The day that young couple walked away from school with their books for the last time, many students came to that teacher and apologized for the way they had laughed at her advice. She shed tears as she told her class, "It is because I am older and can see the glorious future, that I have tried to guide you in the ways of purity."

If our visions keep us pure, our ambitions will make us enterprising and all will fill us with hope. The life that is luminous is the one filled with hope, love and faith.

When you commune with someone a great deal then you become like that person. I know a family with just one little child, a girl. She adores her father, so she tries to imitate him in every way. If he is writing she has to have her pencil and paper and try to write also. Before her little hands were strong enough to carry a clip board she would try to get her father's each time he put it down and after she ruined a few pages of work he bought her a clip board and placed it on a low table.

If we commune with God we grow more like God. The secret of a luminous life is communion with God. What are the results of a life lived in communion with God? First, I would say it is a life of blessing to others. Jesus said, of those who have shining lives: "Ye are the light of the world: let your light so shine, that others, seeing your good works, may glorify your Father who is in heaven."

## BEING BUSY

If you were busy being kind
Before you knew it you would find
You'd soon forget to think 'twas true
That someone was unkind to you.

If you were busy being glad
And cheering people who are sad,
Although your heart might ache a bit,
You'd soon forget to notice it.

If you were busy being good
And doing just the best you could
You'd not have time to blame some man
Who's doing just the best he can.

If you were busy being true
To what you know you ought to do,
You'd be so busy you'd forget
The blunders of the folks you've met.

If you were busy being right
You'd find yourself too busy quite
To criticize your neighbor long
Because he's busy doing wrong.

—Unknown

The luminous life is available to all, that is, all who are willing to pay the price. It is no secret the person you enjoy seeing come into a room or a crowd of people is a person who's life is shining with hope—a life filled with love and visions of good that can be done for those around.

Life was not easy for Moses, he loved the people he led so much that at one time when God would have wiped them out for their sins he said, "Take me also."

Go out today determined to bring blessings to men. To live a pure life even if it means at times standing alone when the crowd pulls the wrong way. The world always needs strong leaders but you do not become a strong leader just by wishing, you pay a price by being useful, unselfish and unwilling to gain success by trampling on others.

"And Moses was with the Lord forty days and forty nights,
.... And Moses' face shone while he talked with him."

Go out from this happy day in your lives determined to walk close to God. You will find happiness, service, and a life that glows for all about to find the way of happiness also.

# 14

# Independence Day

*"With a great sum obtained I this freedom. And Paul said, But I was free born."—Acts 22:28*

### A CALL TO PATRIOTS

In days long gone God spake unto our sires:
  "Courage! Launch out! A new world build for me!"
Then to the deep they set their ships and sailed
  And came to land and prayed that here might be
A realm from pride and despotism free,
A place of peace, the home of liberty.

Lo, in these days to all good men and true
  God speaks again: "Launch out upon the deep
And win for me a world of righteousness!"
  Can we, free men, at such an hour still sleep?
O God of freedom, stir us in our night
That we set forth, for justice, truth and right!
                        —Thomas Curtis Clark

What does the Fourth of July mean to you? If you are my age or older you can remember the old-time Fourth of July picnics. All the county came together at some park and the politicians all were given a chance to speak. I never listened to the politicians but oh, how I did enjoy riding on the merry-go-round, eating cotton candy and just running about in general, getting dirty.

# INDEPENDENCE DAY

The Fourth of July picnics had a deeper meaning. I was just too young to know. They represented the freedom of our great land, freedom of speech, freedom of religion and the right to live as we pleased.

It cost our forefathers to make the matchless Declaration of Independence. Those forty-six men did not underestimate the danger they were facing. They had a great view of the distant generations, the ones who in the future would be free.

After the Declaration of Independence was signed, I can picture the men, some jubilant; some a little awed at the step they had taken; some afraid for their families. Old Ben Franklin issued a word of warning; "We must all hang together, or we shall all hang separately."

A great amount of the trouble in our nation today stems from the fact that Christians have forgotten to "hang together."

Recently a small town near here tried to vote out liquor. The Christian people did their best to rally forces but a man, who belongs to a church, was in a position to make a rule that turned the tide of the vote in favor of liquor. He ruled people could spend a day in that little town and then vote. Wet forces from far away came to town and people who stood for the right were helpless.

Liberty carries with it some ideals. Americans are a liberty-loving people. Have we grown lazy and unwilling to be a really free land. In 1944 I lived with my three children in a small town. My husband was a Chaplain serving in Italy. We were not the least bit afraid at night. We usually latched our screen at night but if it was forgotten we did not feel afraid. Now things are quite different. Our laws are growing more and more lax. We read of people being murdered at home. We lock and double lock our doors each night. If Christians would hang together and demand firmer laws we would get action and be free from fear.

Are we taking liberties with liberty? Are we endangering the lives of others in order to do as we please? People have marched and carried banners. One young person even went so far as to set himself on fire in front of the Pentagon building, protesting war. We read each day about wild, drunk drivers killing and crippling people and we sit still and say nothing.

If we are free we have some obligations to keep. We should obey the laws of the land. We should work to have good laws.

A family with four children attends our church. They are well-behaved children and an honor to their parents. I asked the father why his children were so nice.

"I demand obedience," he smiled. "I am not perfect but I do have more experience. I will make mistakes but as long as they put their feet under my table I expect to be obeyed."

Does America expect to go on putting her feet under God's table and never obeying Him? We think we are the richest nation in the world yet God with a wave of his hand could wipe out all our plenty.

Every bad, disobedient child is a disgrace to his parents. Every citizen who breaks the laws of the land is a disgrace to our country. Every child of God who fails to obey God is a disappointment to those about.

Some years ago we made a trip to the East and stopped late in the afternoon to see the Liberty Bell. The bell is in Independence Hall, in Philadelphia. Behind the hall is a nice little park with very old and huge trees. The park was attractive and many people were sitting on the benches enjoying the cool shade. We did not care to linger there, we wanted so much to see the Liberty Bell. We wanted to see the crack. We pictured in our minds the time when the people met to hear the Declaration of Independence read, then rang the great bell. We pictured the men in a great rush in 1777 when the British occupied Philidelphia, they dumped the bell into the Delaware River.

In Leviticus 25:10 we read, "Proclaim liberty throughout all the land unto all the inhabitants thereof."

To keep our liberty we must be loyal. Many young men have given their lives in battle because they were loyal to

INDEPENDENCE DAY

their country. As Christians are we loyal to our cause? Are we willing to pay the price of obedience and loyalty to have a Christian land?

A third thing to have if we would be free is dependence. Dependence on God who gave us this land, who guided our forefathers in the way to make it free and great. Often, in West Texas we have times when it looks as if we will never see rain again. Then people begin to meet and pray for rain. We have prayer for rain in a very serious way. Our great wheat and cotton crops would fail if God withdrew his protecting hand. We must be dependent to be free!

### WHAT MAKES A NATION GREAT?

Not serried ranks with flags unfurled,
Not armoured ships that gird the world,
Not hoarded wealth nor busy mills,
Not cattle on a thousand hills,
Not sages wise, nor schools nor laws,
Not boasted deeds in freedom's cause—
All these may be, and yet the state
In the eye of God be far from great.

The land is great which knows the Lord,
Whose songs are guided by His Word,
Where justice rules, twix man and man,
Where love controls in art and plan,
Where breathing in his native air,
Each soul finds joy in praise and prayer—
Thus may our country good and great,
Be God's delight—man's best estate.

—Alexander Blackburn

If we obey the laws, if we are loyal to our country, if we depend upon a great God, then we will give time, strength and money to keep our independence.

# 15

# Keep America Beautiful

*"And thy renown went forth among the heathen for thy beauty: for it was perfect through my comeliness, which I had put upon thee, saith the Lord God."—Ezekiel 16:14*

## AMERICA THE BEAUTIFUL

O beautiful for spacious skies,
  For amber waves of grain,
For purple mountain majesties
  Above the fruited plain!

America! America!
  God shed His grace on thee,
And crown thy good with brotherhood,
  From sea to shining sea!

O beautiful for pilgrim feet,
  Whose stern, impassioned stress
A thoroughfare for freedom beat
  Across the wilderness!

America! America!
  God mend thine every flaw,
Confirm thy soul in self-control,
  Thy liberty in law!

O beautiful for heroes proved
  In liberating strife,
Who more than self their country loved,
  And mercy more than life.

# KEEP AMERICA BEAUTIFUL

> America! America!
> May God thy gold refine,
> Till all success be nobleness,
> And every gain divine!
>
> O beautiful for patriot dream
> That sees beyond the years
> Thine alabaster cities gleam,
> Undimmed by human tears!
>
> America! America!
> God shed His grace on thee,
> And crown thy good with brotherhood,
> From sea to shining sea!
> —Kathrine Lee Bates (1904)

When Kathrine Lee Bates wrote her famous poem she had little thought that in a few years the young manhood of America would march and fight on foreign shores for the Beautiful America. She lived to see the day when her song was sung in all the public schools of our land. She was, in her own right, a great educator and writer but I doubt if anything she wrote has shaped young lives as much as "America the Beautiful."

Now as I sit writing, I am well past fifty but goose pimples come as I think of the grand old sing songs we had in high school assembly services. We could lift the roof with that song, and many of my classmates went out in World War II to give their lives for a better America.

The power of Christian purpose will keep our nation beautiful in a spiritual way. When our Pilgrim fathers landed on American shores they saw no beautiful skyline, showing tall sky scrapers and monuments against a setting sun. They saw a land that represented the beauty of freedom.

Our land has been made beautiful by the selfless lives of men gone on in history. George Bancroft, a historian, wrote, "Every enterprise of the pilgrims began from God."

Not long ago I was speaking to a group in a high school. I mentioned that our forefathers were deeply religious and founded our nation on belief in God. A sharp young man came up to me and said, "How do we know they were not like the politicians we hear so much about, feathering their nests with other bird's feathers?"

I will not try to describe the feeling of revulsion which went through me for a moment.

"Can you picture a man like George Washington kneeling in the snow and praying for God to give the men food and clothes?" I retorted quickly.

In II Samuel 3:12 we read; "Whose is the land?"

In Psalm 24:1, we find the answer, "The earth is the Lord's."

I am afraid that in our panic to get wealth and be a strong nation in a military way we have forgotten to teach our young, "The earth is the Lord's." Only as we realize this can we keep our nation beautiful spiritually.

In the twentieth century we have seen the rise of many new nations. The great World War II served to awaken the sleeping millions in Africa and Asia and to arouse in them a desire for freedom and self-rule.

Whether we like it or not many downtrodden nations of the world are rising to fight and die, if need be to make their nations free. We quibble and fuss over how our country is being run; over the part we are playing in the world politics.

At a public dinner in 1816 Stephen Decatur said, "My country may she ever be right, but right or wrong, my country."

But in 1872 an eminent Senator said: "Our country, right or wrong, when right; to be kept right; when wrong; to be put right."

# 16

# Travel in Strange Places

*"In the days of Shamgar the son of Anath, In the days of Jael, the highways were unoccupied, and the travellers walked through byways."—Judges 5:6*

Because of the insecurity of the country at the time this poem was written people were afraid to use the main highways. The great trade routes were empty and the life of the people in the country was stagnated. The people of Israel were in a down-trodden condition. The obscure and dangerous hidden paths were the only means of communication.

As we travel through this world there are times when fear makes us travel in strange places. Fear makes us take short cuts we would best leave untraveled.

### ASPIRATIONS

Our aims are all too high; we try
    To gain the summit at a bound,
When we should reach it step by step,
    And climb the ladder round by round.
He who would climb the heights sublime,
    Or breathe the purer air of life,
Must not expect to rest in ease,
    But brace himself for toil or strife.

## PLEASE GIVE A DEVOTION—for All Occasions

We should not in our blindness seek
  To grasp alone for grand and great,
Disdaining every smaller good,—
  For trifles make the aggregate.
And if a cloud should hover o'er
  Our weary pathway like a pall,
Remember God permits it there,
  And his good purpose reigns o'er all.

Life should be full of earnest work,
  Our hearts undashed by fortune's frown;
Let perseverance conquer fate,
  And merit seize the victor's crown.
The battle is not to the strong,
  The race not always to the fleet;
And he who seeks to pluck the stars,
  Will lose the jewels at his feet.
                              —Anonymous

A sad story was told in the papers a few years ago about a family in the far west who started out for an afternoon drive. The mountains were beautiful and the day pleasant. They saw a strange road leading away from the main highway, so they decided to follow it for awhile. When they had gone a number of miles something went wrong with the car. They could not remember seeing any houses on the road, nor had they passed or met any cars. The father started walking back in the direction of the main highway. The family remained in the car. Several days later the body of the man was found, he had died from the desert heat. The rest of the family were very ill for a number of days suffering from dehydration. They were fortunate an old prospector came down the road and found them.

We may at times be forced, as were the children of Israel, to take the back roads and the byroads, to travel in strange places, but we must know where we are planning to go. If we are sure the goal is out there at the end of the strange path then we can journey on.

A young man from a popular college in Texas went to New York City to try for a job. He traveled a strange path in

74

the city. He wanted the job so very much that when he was tempted by the interviewer to take a drink he did so. Not stopping with one the two decided to go to a hotel and really make a night of reveling and drinking. The interviewer and the interviewed both became very drunk. One thing led to another and they began to fight. The strange path the young college man took that night led to the death of the interviewer. The strange path led to months in jail, to a good name ruined, to a job lost. If he had only been able to say, "No, I do not care to drink." One man would be alive today, and he would have a better chance at success in life.

> Two men trod the way of life;
> The first with downcast eye
> The second with an eager face
> Uplifted to the sky.
>
> He who gazes upon the ground
> Said, "Life is dull and grey,"
> But he who looked unto the stars
> Went singing on his way.
> —Selected

There are a few strange paths we can name which will be best to leave untrod: harboring bitterness in our soul toward God or man is a path to avoid; imagining that people are not our friends just because we do not follow in the same paths they pursue; wasting time on being peevish and spoiled; worrying when we are doing the best we can; thinking evil of friends when we do not have the facts.

> I sought to hear the voice of God.
> And climbed the topmost steeple,
> But God declared: "Go down again—
> I dwell among the people.
> —Unknown

Then there are strange paths that we may well tread and lead to more victorious living. At his inauguration John F. Kennedy said; "Let us go forth to lead the land we love."

PLEASE GIVE A DEVOTION—for All Occasions

A friend of mine was very good in high school. He was a born leader. I knew him because he organized a Morning Watch in his school and asked me to be one of the speakers. As graduation drew near he wanted very much to attend a religious college. The only one where he was able to obtain a scholarship was a thousand miles from his hometown.

"I hate to go so far from home, but it is an opportunity I must take." He bravely went away to tread strange paths. When he came home for Christmas his face was radiant and he was a very happy boy.

"How have you managed to be so happy so far from home for four months?" I asked.

"I am helping in a small church on Sundays, I sing and direct the youth activities." He looked ten feet tall as he said, "I have had moments of homesickness but being busy helping others helps get by those moments."

He went to walk in strange paths but he did not forget the things he had been taught to love and respect; the kind of life he had been brought up to live.

There will always be some strange paths in life. Every day is a new and different day from the one just past. The important problem with Christians is: how may I best walk through today and serve my Lord most.

All paths, strange or familiar, have some shadows, some perils. If we keep our faces toward the sunshine of God's love as we walk, the shadows of doubt and fear will fall behind us.

Not always can I see the course
My ship of life must sail;
But since my Father guides the helm
I'll calmly face the gale.

—Selected

76

# 17

# Vacation for God or from God

*"It is of the Lord's mercies that we are not consumed, because his compassions fail not. They are new every morning: great is thy faithfulness."*
—*Lamentations 3:22, 23*

Don't you just love to start planning for vacation time? Not all people are fortunate enough to have a vacation each year. Most of America finds time for a few days off from regular work. Statistics tell us a great majority of Americans spend their days off at vacation time driving someplace in the family car.

However we go, by plane, train, car or bus, or even if we just walk to the local park, we should take someone with us.

"Oh, I like to go off all alone," some people say.

"We like to take an extra child because we have only one," some parents tell me.

"We like to be alone because we work with people all the year except vacation."

We could write pages on the different ways people want to spend vacation days. I want to bring out the fact that wherever we go, whatever we do, we should not fail to take Christ with us.

A story coming out of World War II is about as follows:

The dean of a college in the Philippines, Buenaventura Bello, a very small man physically, was seated at his desk in the college when the enemy stormed in.

The leader of the group ordered him to walk over to the American and Filipino flags on the wall and tear them down.

"If you want the flags down, you will do it yourself," Bello told the man.

Later he told the thought that went through his mind as that cruel man drew a revolver and shot him.

"There are moments in the lives of men when they are impelled to certify—to seal—with their actions what they believe and what they teach. Such a moment has now arrived in my life. I shall so certify."

When we get up each new day we should say to ourselves, "Today I shall certify by my actions and deeds that I love Christ."

Many people, when packing for vacation, never think to pack or place in the car a Bible. They say, "Let's just forget it all until we get home, just relax."

What if God relaxed that week and withdrew His protecting care from your life? You would never return home safely!

Vacations are wonderful and I am for them, but not vacations from God. Vacations with God are much better.

There is no place you can go that is so far away or so sorry that you cannot see the love of God if you look for it.

Many years ago a family from our church in East Texas, made a long trip to California. At that time a trip across such a long dry country was something special, at least for common folks.

When they came back we all asked questions. Where did you stop? What did you see, and eat?

"Did you gamble in Reno?" someone asked as a joke.

"We went inside one of those places, just to see." The woman told us. "We were so excited and so fascinated we stayed a long time. I looked toward the street where we had left our four children in the car, the children were all lined up on their knees, with faces pressed against the glass looking in."

We were staring at her in amazement.

"I told my husband, 'Let's get out of here, a place not fit for our children is not fit for us."

When you go on vacation don't spend time in places not suitable for Christ to go with you.

### VISION

No vision and you perish,
    No ideal and you're lost;
Your heart must ever cherish
    Some faith at any cost;
Some hope, some dream to cling to,
    Some rainbow in the sky,
Some melody to sing to,
    Some service that is high.
                    —H. du Autremont

From time to time some smart person brings out an idea such as, "God Is Dead," or "God Is a Myth."

Oh, how sorry I feel for such people, they surely have never had a vacation in the mountains, or on the banks of a great river, or sailing on the ocean!

How can you explain the soaring peaks, the deep gorge, the many colored rocks, the giant trees without taking God along?

### GIVE

See the rivers flowing
    Downward to the sea,
Pouring all their treasures
    Bountiful and free:
Yet to help their giving
    Hidden springs arise;
Or, if need be, showers
    Feed them from the skies!

Watch the princely flowers
　　Their rich fragrance spread,
Load the air with perfumes,
　　From their beauty shed:
Yet their lavish spending
　　Leaves them not in dearth,
With fresh life replenished
　　By their mother earth!

Give thy heart's best treasures,
　　From fair Nature learn;
Give thy love—and ask not,
　　Wait not a return!
And the more thou spendest
　　From thy little store,
With a double bounty
　　God will give thee more.
　　　　　　　—Adelaide Procter

Some friends were on a vacation in the great city of Atlanta, Georgia. They went to church and sat by a lady they had never seen before nor would ever see again. She was so impressed by them that she offered them free lodging at her home while they were in the city. They did not accept the offer but they had a warm glow in their hearts just knowing that Christians love Christians even in strange places.

When we are on vacation my husband makes it a habit to ask the people at motel offices and the ones who service the car, "Where do you go to church?"

Many times they say, "I am too busy to go."

Then he tries to witness to them about God's great care and love. Sometimes they tell him enthusiastically about their church and pastor. Then at times they say, "My wife and children go, I work."

As we vacation we can relax and still work for God. We can still attend services and travel all we need to on a trip. Sometimes at services people tell us of some local sight we need to see and we reap a little extra bonus by going to see something different.

# 18

# The Blessing of Work

*"... we command and exhort by our Lord Jesus Christ, that with quietness they work, and eat their own bread. But ye, brethren, be not weary in well doing."*
—*II Thessalonians 3:12, 13*

### HIS WORK REQUIRETH HASTE

It's such a shame each day to live
   In idleness and waste,
When God calls us our best to give,
   And he requireth haste!

God's service we should never shirk,
   Though such might please our taste,
For God has made each for his work,
   Which still requireth haste.

We ought to serve the Lord each day,
   Our thoughts, our deeds all chaste;
We ought to tell men of the Way,
   And bear the news in haste.

Procrastination bids us wait,
   Though Christ our duty traced,
And sin still tempts us with its bait,
   But God still bids us haste!

## PLEASE GIVE A DEVOTION—for All Occasions

> The judgment day will surely come,
> When we through life have raced,
> And then our mouths will be struck dumb,
> Because we made no haste.
>
> —J. T. Bolding

Isn't it wonderful to get up in the morning, eat a good breakfast and go about the work you enjoy doing! It is a blessing we take for granted and fail to say thank you to God for it.

As I go about visiting for my church I often meet people who have been very active but are now too old to work, they are doomed to merely sit and be waited upon.

Often an elderly person will say, "Oh, if I just had the strength to work as I once did."

There are people on long waiting lists wanting to come to America because they feel that here they can work and feed their families. Work is a blessing.

A young man who grew angry with his job resigned. It was several months before he could get another church. Often as he prayed during that time he would say, "If my foresight were as good as my hindsight I would not make so many mistakes."

Work is a blessing sent from God to keep people busy, to make people useful, to keep people from being bored with life. People who work are usually happy people.

Longfellow wrote:

> The heights of great men reached and kept
> Were not attained by sudden flight,
> But they, while their companions slept,
> Were toiling upward in the night.

Many people want to be great, to have big places but they are unwilling to go up the ladder round by round. This is the age of space and flying. Some people think they can just bypass the lowly places and fly to the top. Someone in jest has said, "They want the key to the presidential wash room, but not the dirt and grime one accumulates climbing to the office of president."

# THE BLESSING OF WORK

It is the duty of parents to teach their children to work, to know the joy of a task accomplished.

Work is not a narcotic but it sure will make one feel needed and useful in the world. In New Testament times, as today, there were people who wanted to live off the labor of others. The problem was so great Paul wrote in II Thessalonians 3:10, " . . . that if any would not work, neither should he eat."

Abraham Lincoln said, "As labor is the common burden of our race, so the effort of some to shift their shares of the burden on to the shoulders of others is the great durable curse of the race."

Today you could not stand on any street corner and chat very long before someone would say, "It looks as though a few will have to work and feed the rest of the nation."

Work is a blessing given us from God. We cannot make all men equal for all do not want to be equal. Often a friend will say, "Oh I think I will write a book, I can if you did."

I always answer, "Yes I am sure you could."

That friend does not take into account that I spend long hours, praying, reading, and studying before I even start a book.

Tolstoy wrote, "The happiness of men consists in life. And life is in labor."

Horace wrote, "Life grants no boon to man without much toil."

In America we are very proud of what we call Private Enterprise. Well, every family should have some private enterprise. Plans to improve their home, their language, even plans to improve their church by working. Enterprise is a precious ingredient.

There are some things we can develop to make us enjoy work and count it a blessing.

The first might be listed as initative, that ingredient that compels us to want to do something.

Then there is courage. Sometimes a job seems far away and maybe impossible but if we have courage we can do it.

## PLEASE GIVE A DEVOTION—for All Occasions

When my son was a small boy he liked to stand around a small factory where the men made door mats. One day the boss told him he must either learn to make a mat or go home. He was not over ten years old but he made the mat, surprising the boss. The boss gave him the mat as a gift and then sent him home. He had the courage to try and he was very proud of that door mat.

Resourcefulness was a trait Americans inherited from sturdy forefathers. Are we handing that same gift down to our children?

There are those who work for the joy of seeing a task well done. They do not first stop and ask, "Will I get credit for this?"

They work for the pure joy of achievement. To them the privilege of work is a real blessing. We should seek to work for the joy of work and be thankful for the free land which makes it possible for us to seek the kind of labor we enjoy.

### WORK

Lord, let me not die until
   I've done for thee
My earthly work, whatever it may be.
   Call me not hence
With mission unfulfilled;
   Let me not leave my space of ground
Untilled;
   Impress the truth upon me that not one
Can do the portion that I leave undone.

—Anonymous

# 19

# School Days for Young and Old

*"Learn of me."—Matthew 11:29*

*"It is hard for thee to kick against the pricks."*

*—Acts 26:14*

### A SONG OF SERVICE

If all my pain,
    And all my tears,
And all that I have learnt
    Through all the years,
Could make one single perfect song
    To right some wrong,
To lift some fallen head,
    To light some darkened mind,
I should feel that not in vain
    I served mankind.
                    —Marguerite Few

If we wish to be prepared for life we must have some kind of education. An education opens up the way, keeps people from being at a disadvantage. The better the education the better one is prepared to be a leader, in the working world, in school, in church, in politics. In short, an education prepares one to live better in a modern world.

Paul approved of education in the Scriptures, "Give diligence to present thyself approved unto God, a workman that needeth not to be ashamed, rightly dividing the word of truth" (II Timothy 2:15).

Jesus taught a school for grown people. He said, "Learn of me."

I think those pupils of Jesus were a representative group of a classroom today. There was an impulsive one, Peter. There were passionate ones like James and John. There are always some unselfish ones like Andrew. Then there are the greedy ones like Judas.

How discouraged Jesus must have grown at times, such as the night he prayed in the Garden and found them sleeping. How often today he finds us sleeping when we should be awake to the great opportunities about us.

> Childhood's years are passing o'er us;
> Soon our school-days will be done.

When the school days of life are ended life will be over.

In school you remember some teachers more than others. Some are harder to please; some demand better work; some seem to love more. Peter thinking of his days with Christ said, "Leaving us an example, that ye should follow in his steps" (I Peter 2:21).

We, too, have that wonderful example of Christ to follow. We, too, must set an example for those who are learning from us. Our friends, our neighbors, our children, all look to us for examples in ways to live each day. Are we good schoolmasters? Are we good pupils of the one who said, "Learn of me"?

Moffatt translates Ecclesiastes 4:5 as follows: "He is a fool who folds his hands and lets life go to ruin."

September is the time for starting fresh, new school years. People of all ages can take fresh starts in the school of life, any time of the year they are willing to try. Sad to say they cannot call back the years they failed to put forth the effort to succeed and grow.

# SCHOOL DAYS FOR YOUNG AND OLD

## NEVER GIVE UP

There's a time to part and a time to meet,
There's a time to sleep and a time to eat,
There's a time to work and a time to play,
There's a time to sing and a time to pray.
There's a time that's glad and a time that's blue,
There's a time to plan and a time to do,
There's a time to grin and show your grit,
But there never was a time to quit.

—Anonymous

In our wonderful land where almost any youth can go to school, not just a few months or years but until they have a wonderful education, we should all be so thankful. We are neglecting to demand of our youth the better world we should expect from their great opportunities, we are letting them get soft and useless by failing to demand more.

Browning wrote; "Ah, but a man's reach should exceed his grasp, Or what is heaven for?"

We must teach our youth there is something greater to reach up for, something great to reach out and give, and not let them be satisfied until they have reached up and out to the very best of their ability.

# 20

# Discover New Lands

*"Now the Lord has said unto Abram, Get thee out of*
*thy country, and from thy kindred and from thy father's*
*house unto a land that I will show thee."—Genesis 12:1*

Recently I read the story of a girl who had been six feet
seven inches tall. She had never had a date. She felt out of
the world until some doctors decided to try cutting some bone
off her legs and making her only five feet eleven inches tall.
She discovered a new world as she was written about and as
she convalesced. Scores of people wrote her letters and one
young man asked for her first date.

As she was convalescing she learned to accomplish things
such as drawing and painting. "The world is now my friend
in place of my enemy."

Almost all really wonderful and great things come about
because someone is willing to try for something new and
different.

We think of Columbus when we think of October 12. We
think of someone daring to discover new lands for his
queen.

As Christians we should be ever eager to discover new lands
for our Christ.

To discover new lands for Christ we must discover new

followers for him. They can be found on any street in any town where people live, for all have not yet accepted his free gift of salvation.

God called Abram to go to a new land because he wanted him to become the Father of a great nation. He calls us to launch out in new ways, sometimes in new places in order that we may add to that great nation of believers.

> More light shall break from out Thy Word
> For Pilgrim followers of the gleam
> Till led by Thy free Spirit Lord,
> We see and share the Pilgrims dream.

If we would get up and go to the land which God would show us we must first plan to answer God's call. Too many so-called Christians plan to be too busy to answer when called. If we plan to answer we will prepare to be ready when called. We can prepare by reading the Bible, attending services and by growing closer to God.

If we plan and prepare for the discovery of new souls for Christ then we must pray for God to send us out on a mission to win the lost. Pray for Him to fill us with the Spirit and give us success in our endeavor.

Colombus did not just suddenly spring into a great discovery. He made some trips to close places, England, Genoa, Chios. He did not set out to find America, only Asia. Most Christians, if they will get up and go to the land the Lord will show them, will discover they have reached far more than they started out to win.

Columbus could never have reached America if he had not first prepared for the voyage. Our success also depends upon our plans and preparations.

Some person made the remark, "Some well-fed bodies house undernourished souls."

We cannot start out to discover new lands until we have well-fed souls spiritually.

We must not be afraid of striving for what seems unattainable. Columbus sought a way to reach a known land by a new route. Abram started for a strange land with God for his guide. We, too, will have God for our companion and guide if we start at his orders.

Then there is the big problem of decision. We must purpose in our hearts that we will discover new lands for God.

### DECISIONS

When in doubt about decisions
  Which you are called upon to make,
You might well defer your answer
  While a second look you take.

If you're doubtful of the rightness
  Of the project in your mind,
Maybe you should reconsider
  'Til a better you can find.

If you're tempted oft to purchase
  Things which are of doubtful need,
Note, it's easy to say, "Charge it,"
  But the paying's rough indeed!

Things which seem of vast importance
  At this present point in time,
May soon lose their use and glamour
  And seem hardly worth a dime.

It's just fine to make decisions:
  With your right ones be not late,
But with wrong ones be not hasty:
  Make them right or make them wait.
  —J. T. Bolding

Did you ever walk into a store and see a table loaded down with boxes all wrapped up and a sign saying: "Your choice, fifty cents." I have to make myself turn and walk out because I just have the strongest urge to buy one of those boxes just to see what is inside.

God put in most humans a desire to see what is unknown to us. To go to strange places, to try new dishes, to wear new kinds of clothes. We are a people who like to discover! Second

90

## DISCOVER NEW LANDS

Corinthians 9:6 says, "He which soweth sparingly shall reap also sparingly; and he which soweth bountifully shall reap also bountifully."

Do not expect to go out and discover new lands for the Lord without working. This is a world of constant new discoveries but we get none of them for nothing. We must be willing to make sacrifices as Abram had to leave his kinfolks. Sometimes we must sacrifice spending lots of time just sitting and visiting with relatives when God needs us for bigger things.

### HOME

On any morning—
Think of stepping on shore
And finding it Heaven!
Of taking hold of a hand
And finding it God's hand;
Of breathing a new air
And finding it celestial air;
Of feeling invigorated
And finding it immortality;
Of passing from storm and tempest
To an unknown calm;
Of waking up and finding it Home!
—Selected

What a wondrous land to discover!

# 21

# Andrew the Discoverer of Men

*"He first findeth his own brother Simon, and saith unto him, We have found the Messias which is being inter-preted, the Christ."—John 1:41*

*"One of his disciples, Andrew, Simon Peter's brother, saith unto him, There is a lad here, which hath five barley loaves, and two small fishes: but what are they among so many?"—John 6:8, 9*

### MY FRIEND

My friend is such a blessed joy,
As faithfully he stands
Encouraging my fearful heart
Amid earth's shifting sands;
To me his life is like the loaves
And fishes in Christ's hands.
—J. T. Bolding

I read a story about a female duck on a ranch. The duck was wild and it was time for the duck to fly South. This duck could not fly because of a broken wing. As she waddled along she was not alone, her mate walked at her side urging her on and refusing to take flight until she did.

Wouldn't you like a friend like that. One who thought of you first and himself later? That is how God loves us. Even when we are broken and unable to go on He still urges and helps us along.

Very little is said of Andrew in the Bible yet we know he was the type who thought of others first. How happy he must have been when Christ called him to follow, yet he knew his brilliant, impetuous brother Simon would make a great disciple. He did not say, "Now I will be ahead of Simon for once in our life. I have been called first."

No, much as Andrew wanted to go right along with Christ, he ran first to get his brother and bring him to Jesus.

"A lot of folks I know would choose a million bucks to spend, but if I had to make my choice I'd rather have a friend. Oh, spending money may be fun and mighty well worth trying, but spending time with someone nice is much more satisfying. Some people think that fame must be life's greatest dividend, but give me, if I have my choice, a faithful, life-long friend. For fame and money get away, and leave you high and stranded; but once you've found a real true friend you're never empty handed."—Selected

What a wonderful friend Andrew must have been to all who knew him. He was not looking for the best place for himself but constantly seeking to lead others to follow Jesus.

When he came to tell Jesus about the little lad with the loaves and fishes he had probably been talking to the lad earlier maybe taking time to explain to him the words Jesus was saying. He probably told him of some of the great miracles he had seen Jesus perform. At any rate he had made a friend of the lad.

Leading others to Jesus is not restricted to Andrew. All God's children have a duty to perform in winning others, in helping others, in improving life for those who are in need.

A young man named Tommy went to Wayland Baptist College. He had been blind since the age of six. His greatest joy came from his friends and their telling him about the world.

He was making slow progress in Wayland because he could not write his Braille notes as fast as the teachers talked.

An ex-sailor in the school took fifteen dollars out of his pocket and started a fund for a tape recorder for Tommy. All the students helped a little and finally the big day arrived. Wayland is just a small school and most everyone knows the problems of the others. Tommy was led to the stage during the chapel services and presented the tape recorder. No one was ashamed of the tears they shed that morning nor of the few cents they had contributed. Tommy could now make his grades without the aid of writing so much.

To me that ex-sailor, going to school on a G.I. Bill was an Andrew. As a gas station attendant said to my husband, "He seen a need and he filled it."

### JUST FOLKS

I've watched them grow from boys to men,
　But down the years I've never known
A lad to be successful when
　He had to stand to life alone.

No one can overcome the odds
　Without a friendly helpful hand.
Somewhere along the road he plods,
　Youth needs a man to understand.

Who thinks to live his life alone
　Must meet, no matter where he fares,
The faith and hope just like his own
　Another on the sideline shares.

We are a part of all we know.
　Success and failure touch men all;
They thrill with pride when strength we show
And they are saddened when we fall.
　　　　　　　　　　—Edgar A. Guest

Andrew went forth to seek other men who could perhaps shine brighter than he. I have known pastors who wanted credit for all they did in the church. Then, I have known pastors who constantly worked to develop their members into good leaders. There are so many people just sitting idle, needing to be developed and grown for Christ work.

Has someone new moved across the street or down the block, even next door? Can you go to Christ in prayer and say, "I have discovered a lad, a man, a woman, here in need of your love"? Then go in the strength of the Holy Spirit and bring that soul to Christ.

Not all can be leaders and bright lights in the church but I am persuaded all can be Andrews and help discover talent and ability in others.

You must first become a searcher. Search for those in need of the Lord. Then become a friend to those persons. Then ask them to go with you.

While visiting we had to wait in the living room of the home for the lady of the house to dress. A neighbor lady, in her fifties, was answering the door. After we introduced ourselves we began to talk. We found that the neighbor was not a Christian; had not been to church since she was eighteen years old. She felt justified because there was no church of her mother's faith in our city, so she didn't go any place. We tried to be Andrews and urged her to come; at least to visit our services.

Being a discoverer of men for Christ and being a friend seems to me to go hand and hand.

Andrew loved his brother, so he sought to bring him to Christ. If you love your neighbor you will seek to bring them to Christ.

## 22

# Thankfulness a Habit

*"What shall I render unto the Lord for all his benefits towards me?"—Psalm 116:12*

*"I will bless the Lord at all times, his praise shall continually be in my mouth."—Psalm 14:1*

### GOD'S BOUNTIES

For morning and the hopes of day,
For hours to work and hours to play,
For courage and contentment here,
For trust to strengthen, joy to cheer—
  We praise thee, Lord!

For evening and the duties done,
For every strife of conscience won,
For hours to dream and hours to rest,
For all through love made manifest—
  We bless thee, Lord!

For home and those who love us there,
For friends and kindred everywhere,
For life. and for the life to be,
Eternal fellowship, with thee—.
  We thank thee, Lord!

                —Unknown

We should not wait until Thanksgiving Day to bless and

# THANKFULNESS A HABIT

thank our God. Each day we should make it a habit of life to enter into his courts with thanksgiving and praise.

Think of all the wonderful things for which we should be grateful. We should be most grateful if we have good health, strength and sanity. We should make it a habit to be thankful for our friends and neighbors. It doesn't even hurt to tell them how glad we are to have them for friends.

We should thank God for our relatives, if they are good. If they are not the kind we can be proud of, we might try helping them improve.

Sometimes we fail to appreciate life's blessings until they are taken from us. If we make a habit of being thankful we will not have to resort to the old adage: "You never miss the water until the well runs dry."

We must be grateful for our temporal blessings: our houses, cars, furniture, good food and clothes. We should thank God for letting us live in a land where there is plenty if one is willing to work. We should be thankful for our form of government for without it we might find life much harder.

There are times in all lives when we feel we are being tried but isn't it wonderful that God cares enough about his children to test and try them at times. I remember a little boy who was very jealous for his mother's attention. At times when she had company he would act naughty. She became exasperated one day when a friend was visiting who had a little girl just his age. At last the mother took him to the bathroom and administered a sound spanking. When he returned he took the little girl to the playroom and was a perfect little gentleman.

"I guess your mother doesn't care much for you if she doesn't spank you often." He was heard telling the girl.

Sometimes when we get away from the habit of thankfulness God has to spank us to make us remember our blessings and his love.

It is so easy in times of much prosperity and rich harvests to forget to thank God for the unspeakable gift of His love.

For Jesus Christ and the Holy Spirit are so near to us at all times.

When we realize we should thank God even for the sunshine and the rain, we feel humble and our hearts are filled with humility.

How can we make thanksgiving in our hearts anything less than a daily habit.

God has the habit of goodness and forgiveness, so we in turn must have the habit of thanksgiving.

"I will bless the Lord at all times, his praise shall continually be in my mouth" (Psalm 14:1).

On a subway train in New York a poor cripple woman was almost mashed by those standing next to her. Her crippled leg was hurting and she longed to be home. A man holding the strap near her looked down and complained that some always managed to get seats. The woman looked back and with a sweet smile replied, "I will give you my seat and my cripple leg for your two good ones."

The man felt ashamed. The men who stood near and heard felt thankful for their good strong legs and the tiredness seemed to fly away. None wanted to trade.

We must make a habit of counting our blessings. We must be habitually grateful for the riches of God's bounty to us.

In the twenty-third Psalm David said, "My cup runneth over."

Most of us if we could take a trip in some impoverished lands would indeed cry, "My cup runneth over."

### MURMURING

Some murmur when their sky is clear
And wholly brought to view,
If one small speck of dark appears
In their great heaven of blue;
And some with thankful love are filled
If but one streak of light,
One ray of God's good mercy, gild
The darkness of their night.

# THANKFULNESS A HABIT

In palaces are hearts that ask,
  In discontent and pride,
Why life is such a dreary task
  And all good things denied
And hearts in poorest huts admire
  How love has in their aid
(Love that never seems to tire)
  Such rich provision made.

                    —Author unknown

# 23

# The Extra Blessings of Thanksgiving

*"Freely ye have received, freely give."—Matthew 10:8*

*"It is a good thing to give thanks unto the Lord."*
*—Psalm 92:1*

*"Were there not ten cleansed, but where are the nine?"*
*—Luke 17:17*

### THOUGHTFUL THANKSGIVING

For sunlit hours and visions clear,
For all remembered faces dear,
For comrades of a single day,
Who sent us stronger on our way,
For friends who shared the year's long road
And bore with us the common load,
For hours that levied heavy tolls,
But brought us nearer to our goals,
For insights won through toil and tears,
We thank Thee, Keeper of our years.
—Author unknown

Sarah Hale was the lady responsible for Thanksgiving becoming a national holiday. Perhaps you have never heard her name. She was the editor of a woman's magazine in Philadelphia. She sent letters to all the governors of the states and territories. She asked them to set apart the last Thursday in November for a national Thanksgiving Day. She was disappointed that so few paid any attention to her but year after year she kept writing. Finally after the battle of Gettysburg she wrote to President Lincoln.

President Lincoln set aside a special day for the national holiday of thanksgiving. Since that time each president sets aside a special day for thanksgiving.

Taking time once a year to offer thanksgiving brings a nation to the remembrance of one who is the giver of all bountiful harvest. It brings the blessings of thankfulness to each heart. Pausing each day in the home or office will bring a blessing of thankfulness.

This morning when I awoke the sun was shining just a little peep in the East. The sky was so beautiful I thanked God for the hopes of a lovely day. After I got up I enjoyed a good breakfast and before I ate it my husband and I together thanked God for it. The time I took for thanksgiving I do not miss and I feel so much happier.

A popular magazine carried the story of a famous man who often got out of bed and made everyone around him miserable. If he had gotten out of bed praising God he would have been happier and it would have been easier to work with him.

### THANK GOD FOR LIFE

Thank God for life!
E'en though it bring much bitterness and strife,
And all our fairest hopes be wrecked and lost,
E'en though there be more ill than good in life,
We cling to life and reckon not the cost.
Thank God for life!

Thank God for love!
For though sometimes grief follows in its wake,
Still we forget love's sorrow in love's joy,
And cherish tears with smiles for love's dear sake;
Only in heaven is bliss without alloy.
Thank God for love!

Thank God for pain!
No tear hath ever yet been shed in vain,
And in the end each sorrowing heart shall find
No curse, but blessings in the hand of pain;
Even when he smiteth, then is God most kind.
Thank God for pain!

Thank God for death!
Who touches anguished lips and stills their breath
And giveth peace unto each troubled breast;
Grief flies before thy touch, O blessed death;
God's sweetest gift; thy name in heaven is Rest.
Thank God for death!

—Anonymous

"Were there not ten cleansed, but where are the nine?" Even Jesus appreciated people being grateful for the blessings he gave them. Do we take good health as our own special right and forget to thank God for it? Ingratitude causes people to miss so many blessings. It causes their lives to be narrow and little. I like the drapes wide open on a beautiful day so that the sun can come in and fill the room with cheer.

A wide open heart is filled with Jesus' love and likes to let it shine on others.

At Christmastime our grandchildren from California came to spend a few days. The weather was cold but beautiful and clear. The morning they were planning to leave for home we awoke to find it snowing. Of course, my first thought was, "How will you get over the mountains if the snow gets deep?"

"Open the curtains quick," the little boys called. They had never seen snow falling before. They didn't think of much except looking out at the snow the rest of the morning. I actually caught myself being glad it was snowing as I watched them enjoy it so very much.

We miss the blessings of thankful hearts because we so often take our blessings for granted. Some place I read; "Any fool can criticize and complain—and usually does!"

# THE EXTRA BLESSINGS OF THANKSGIVING

How foolish those nine men who went away cleansed but who had not a moment to say "Thank you, Lord."

"Freely ye have received, freely give." We cannot truly be thankful for our own blessings without wanting to give a part of them to others.

Simply being thankful is not enough, we must show our gratitude for blessings by saying "Thank you."

If the two words "Thank you" can make so much difference to us in our relationship to people, think how much difference a grateful heart can make to God.

One time when I was a teen-ager I felt my mother was making more dresses for my younger sister than for me. So childlike I accused her of loving my sister most.

"No I do not love her most but she is so pleased with all the things I make for her," she sighed. "You are hard to please."

Had I shown more gratitude I would have had more dresses.

An old adage reads; "Gratitude is the fairest blossom which springs from the soul; and the heart knoweth none more fragrant."

Will you be one of the nine and go away?

# 24

# How Far to Your Bethlehem?

*"Now when Jesus was born in Bethlehem of Judea in the days of Herod the king, behold, there came wise men from the east to Jerusalem, saying, Where is he that is born King of the Jews? for we have seen his star in the east, and are come to worship him . . . and he sent them to Bethlehem, and said, Go and search diligently for the young child."—Matthew 2:1, 2, 8*

OUR WISH TO YOU

"God bless the master of this house,
The mistress also,
And all the little children
That round the table go.
And all your kin and kinfolks
That dwell both far and near.
I wish you a Merry Christmas
And a happy New Year."
—18th Century Carol

There seems to be a feeling of Christmas in the air. We go about rushing madly. We have forgotten that to really find Christmas we must go to Bethlehem. How far is it?

For Mary the road to Bethlehem must have seemed so very long and tiresome. Her body must have grown weary and

# HOW FAR TO YOUR BETHLEHEM?

fatigued. Perhaps she often strained her eyes looking to see the little town in the distance. There is no doubt the trip was hard for that very night after arriving Mary gave birth to her child—the child that was to draw all men unto him, and cause men to leave homes and loved ones to travel far to tell the story of his birth. How far is it to Bethlehem?

The shepherds knew the distance, yet they left their flocks and hurried there. The wise men knew it would be far but they, too, were willing to go and seek a new King.

### HOW FAR TO BETHLEHEM

"How far is it to Bethlehem town?"
Just over Jerusalem hills adown,
Past lovely Rachel's white-domed tomb—
Sweet shrine of motherhood's young doom.

It isn't far to Bethlehem town—
Just over the dusty roads adown,
Past Wise Men's well, still offering
Cool droughts from welcome wayside spring;
Past shepherds with their flutes of reed
That charm the woolly sheep they lead;
Past boys with kites on hilltops flying,
And soon you're there where Bethlehem's lying.
Sunned white and sweet on olived slopes,
Gold lighted still with Judah's hopes.

And so we find the Shepherd's field
And plain that gave rich Boaz yield;
And look where Herod's villa stood
We thrill that earthly parenthood
Could foster Christ who was all—good;
And thrill that Bethlehem town today
Looks down on Christian homes that pray.

It isn't far to Bethlehem town!
It's anywhere that Christ comes down
And finds in people's friendly face
A welcome and abiding place.
The road to Bethlehem runs right through
The homes of folks like me and you.
                    Madeleine Sweeny Miller

No, it is not far to Bethlehem but we allow so many things to keep us away, to block our path and say, "Stay, wait before you go."

Some of the people who went to worship long ago at that first Christmas season had a long way to go but that did not stop them.

Simeon was old and frail, he was prepared for a heavenly home but he wanted so much to see the new King. He asked God to let him live until he had seen Jesus. Perhaps his body suffered with many of the diseases of old age but he must see the little babe before he was willing to go to his resting place. He did not want to see Jesus out of curosity, but to worship.

Word came to the shepherds and the road seemed short as they rushed to worship. The accompaniment of the angels' song took them over the rough hills and valleys in a hurry.

Do we want to worship at Christmas or are we letting all kinds of things keep us from Bethlehem. The biggest hill in our path is usually indifference and selfishness. We want things for ourselves. The cause of Christ can wait until the Christmas gifts are all bought and paid for. Whose birthday do we celebrate anyway?

### THINGS

Do we ever stand and gaze
In bewildered mental daze,
Thinking life is just a maze,
    of THINGS?

Do we give the very best
Of our strength, our zeal, our zest,
Just to feather our life nest,
    With THINGS?

Then at last there'll come the day
When our life ebbs fast away
And grim death will not delay,
    For THINGS.

# HOW FAR TO YOUR BETHLEHEM?

When we see life reach the end,
Well we know, that 'round the bend,
We can never hope to send,
     Those THINGS.

Think not that it was God's plan
For his own created man
Just to fill up his life span,
     With THINGS.

God gave us a mission great
So let's open love's flood gate,
Never making our best wait,
     On THINGS.
                              —J. T. Bolding

Not only do we let the road to Bethlehem get obstructed with things, we let ambition and antagonism mount up in our hearts until we cannot see the glory of the Christ Child.

The Inn Keeper was so near to the glory of Christ, yet he did not worship. Perhaps he was enjoying the talk and excitement of the crowded inn that night, and pleasure and making money kept him from seeing the King.

"Could I know
That they were so important?
Just the two,
No servants, just a workman sort of man,
Leading a donkey, and his wife thereon
Drooping and pale,—I saw them not myself,
My servants must have driven them away;
But had I seen them,—how was I to know?
Were Inns to welcome stragglers, up and down
In all our towns from Beersheba to Dan
Till He should come? And how were men to know?
There was a sign, they say, a heavenly light
Resplendent: but I had no time for stars,
And there were songs of angels in the air
Out on the hills; but how was I to hear
Amid the thousand clamors of an Inn?
                              —Author unknown

Sometimes even devotion for loved ones can keep us from worshiping at Christmastime. We want the best for them and forget that the best can be found as we teach them the way to the King born in Bethlehem.

Today what keeps you from Bethlehem? Is it far from your heart?

Some men working in an office at Christmastime found a small note tied to their office tree when they started to put it up. Dear Santa: I am a little boy 12 years. I would like a little present as we are very poor and our Santa hasn't enough money for presents this year." It was signed with a boy's name and gave his address, in Canada. The employees of the firm began collecting donations for that boy. They asked the telephone company to check on his family. The telephone company found his father was in a Veteran's hospital and the family in very hard circumstances. Oh, I wish I could have been there when that pitiful little family received that gift of money from a firm in the United States. How near to Bethlehem I would have felt if I could have given some on that gift.

There are many needs around us at Christmas time. We are to push other things aside and help fill those needs. If we have a birthday we want it to be our day. We like to be told we are loved and maybe receive a few little gifts. Can we afford to ignore Christ on his birthday? Can't we take time to say "I love you"?

# 25

# Christmas Lights

*"And, lo, the star ... went before them, till it came and stood over where the young child was."—Matthew 2:9*

"What have you done to my porch?" my husband cried as he looked at a few very small nails I had driven into the wood all around the roof.

"How could we have Christmas lights up unless I drove some nails?" I felt defeated. "Why not just look at how pretty the lights are and not think about the nails?"

Many people are looking at Christmas just the way I wanted him to look at the porch. We see the glory and the tinsel but we fail to remember that Jesus did not stay a babe in the manger, he grew to manhood and suffered from the nails on the cross—the nails of hate and shame when there should have been joy and acceptance.

The Christmas message will never bring the peace and joy we want if we look only at the gifts we can get, at the lights we want to decorate our own front porch. There will be a song of joy for us if we plan to light the way for others to have happiness and peace.

Long ago the shepherds had a light to guide their way to Jesus. Today we must have a light to guide us step by step, not just at Christmastime but all through the year.

"Glory to God in the highest, and on earth peace, good will toward men." The angels sang. Today the song is left for us to sing; the light left for us to shine.

### THE STAR OF BETHLEHEM

The brightest gleam that ever shone
Across the world's dark night
Was not reflected from the throne
Of selfishness or might.
Nor was the torch that led the way
To any diadem.
It was love's gentle, golden ray—
The Star of Bethlehem.

The light that longest shall abide
Among the distant years,
And leave on weary faces dried
The most of human tears,
Is not the glow reflected far
From Splendor's gleaming gem.
It is the light of one lone star—
The Star of Bethlehem.
—Clarence E. Flynn

At Christmastime I saw a very pretty, golden tree. I wanted that tree very much but the price was high, so I passed it by. We talked about enlarging our mission gift we always make in honor of Christ's birthday. Things seemed so high, even food to feed the many we planned to have in for Christmas.

"Let us do something bigger this year," my husband said. "I know what I would like to give. You tell me what you want to give and let us see how close we are."

"I want to give all we gave last year, then half that much more." I told him.

"Exactly what I had thought of."

So we enlarged our gift and I did without the golden Christmas tree. I didn't miss it for all my old decorations looked better than ever before. We did not put up a tree.

Just a few days before Christmas my grandchildren from the country came in and brought a tree they had left over

110

from the past. It looked just like a left-over tree, made of tinsel and foil. When they finished putting it up the room glowed.

"It is not as pretty as our new one but anyway you have a tree." They told me. All during the holidays our home seemed to glow with love and blessings. Even the smallest grandchildren did not quarrel over toys or act jealous. Perhaps the glow in our hearts came from knowing we had put Christ first and our wants second. A mission offering is good any time of the year but it will help a great light to shine in the darkest of heathen lands.

Oh, yes, after Christmas I happened to be in the store and there was the golden tree marked down to half price. I had that much left over but I still did not buy it. Somehow it did not seem so important after the holidays. A week later that same tree was still on the mark-down counter at a fourth of the original price. Now it is high up on my closet shelf waiting for next Christmas. After all, how long can one person resist something.

Most of our generation enjoys light, lights and more lights. Periodically our city publishes a little note about how many mercury vapor lights the city has. Good people usually like light. We like the early morning light with birds singing their wake-up song. We like sunlight on our back when we have had a cold and need its healing power. We like the light of love we see in the eyes of our children. We long to see the light of salvation on the face of the unsaved.

I heard about a man who allowed his family to spend a great deal at Christmas, much of it "charged."

"I sat down after Christmas to review the damage." he said. Many of the toys were already broken or the children were tired of them. The tree was ready to be thrown out. We had all eaten too much rich food and felt a little ill and especially we older ones felt overweight. We had overlooked an old aunt who had no one else to remember her. We had completely blotted out the light of Christmas for her by our greed and thoughtlessness. We had been blind to the needs of those about us and determined to have a big time just for ourselves."

How miserable that man must have been, if he were a Christian, for he seemed to have left out the light of Christ completely.

Christmas is more than just the shouts of loved ones coming for a visit. It is more than the happy laughter of little children with new toys. Christ in you becomes the hope of glory, he is a star of hope.

We need a light of rejoicing as well as a star of hope. "When they saw the star, they rejoiced with exceeding great joy" (Matthew 2:10).

Then there is the light of service. Often it will lead us to places we would not otherwise go. We must serve if we would keep our Christmas lights shining bright.

Then, of course, no string of Christmas lights would be complete without the star, or light, of giving. "For God so loved the world, that he gave his only begotten son" (John 3:16). If God could give so much how can we give so little?

Most of the things we really want in life cannot be wrapped up and placed in a neat package under a tree. We want love, security, loyalty, appreciation and happiness.

### LIGHTS OF CHRISTMAS

Oh, cheery lights of Christmas,
  That gleam from porch and sill,
How happily they carry
  Their message of good will,
From cot and mansion 'glinting
  In crimson and in green,
With rainbow hues their tinting
  The Christmas evergreen.

Above the din of traffic
  The carols rise and soar,
And soon the lights are streaming
  From many an open door;

# CHRISTMAS LIGHTS

Then from the cosy fireside
Come sounds of childish glee,
As happy children 'cluster 'round
The lighted Christmas tree.

Oh, welcome lights of Christmas,
What memories unfold
Along their glowing pathway
Of crimson, green and gold,
And troubled hearts grow lighter
As visions they receive
Of peace and love abiding
In the lights of Christmas Eve.

—Katherine L. Daniher

# 26

# Travel Stains (End of Year)

*"And the door was shut."—Matthew 25:10*

*"He that is washed needeth not save to wash his feet; but is clean every whit."—John 13:10*

The Revised Version refers to the words bathe and wash. We get the picture of a traveler who had had his morning bath then started his day's journey. He had a clean body and a refreshed spirit but as he walked his feet became dusty and dirty. So, when he arrived at his destination he does not need a second bath but he needs only to remove the travel stains which he could not help getting as he traveled.

This makes a happy parable of our journey through life. Those "who are Christ's" have received their great cleansing. When they trusted Christ blood and surrendered their life to him, they were cleansed. We do not need to be saved more than one time but we do travel through a dirty, sinful world and gather some stains along the way. I feel secure in my heart that God has a place for me in his Kingdom because I have trusted Him, yet how will I remove the stains of travel? I will pray constantly and ask forgivness when I make mistakes. I will determine in my heart not to get any more stains than possible and I can rest assured that when I ask God to forgive me and take the sins away he will.

As a little girl my mother would send or take me to Sunday School wearing a nice, clean, starched dress. Sometimes when I returned home that dress was not so clean and fresh. If she said anything about the dress I had a ready answer, "The seats were dirty."

We started the year just passed ready to live as nearly right as we could, but something tells me the world was dusty and sinful. Now as we come to the close, we see some of our mistakes and want to do better next time.

### FAREWELL

Farewell, Old Year, the rustle of whose garment,
　Fragrant with memory, I still can hear;
For all thy tender kindness and thy bounty,
　I drop my thankful tribute on thy bier.

What is in store for me, brave New Year, hidden
　Beneath thy glistening robe of ice and snows?
Are there sweet songs of birds, and breath of lilacs,
　And blushing blooms of June's scent-laden rose?

As silent art thou of the unknown future
　As if thy days were numbered with the dead;
Yet, as I enter thy wide-open portal,
　I cross thy threshold with glad hope, not dread.

To me no pain or fear or rushing sorrow
　Hast thou the power to bring without his will;
And so I fear thee not, O untried morrow!
　For well I know my Father is thy King.

If joy thou bringest, straight to God, the giver,
　My gratitude shall rise, for 'tis his gift;
If sorrow, still, 'mid waves of grief's deep river,
　My trembling heart I'll to my Father lift.

So, hope-lit New Year, with thy joys uncertain,
　Whose unsolved mystery none may foretell,
I calmly trust my God to lift thy curtain;
　Safe in his love, for me 'twill all be well.

　　　　　　　　　　　　　　　　　—Selected

The last of a year is a good time for remembering and forgetting. We can be thankful we have traveled the circle of time and came near the close in good health, happiness and fellowship with friends. As we seek to abolish the travel stains of the past twelve months it will be well to forget the things we let make us angry; the things we let make us say hasty words and hurt others. Ask forgivness and then blot them out of your mind. We forget the rainstorm when the sun is shining, so when bad things are past forget them.

> Build thee more stately mansions,
> O my soul,
> As the swift seasons roll;
> Leave thy low vaulted past.
> —C. R .S.

Soon the door of time will shut on this old year. I hope we will not be like the virgins in the bridal party who waited until the last to secure oil for their lamps. When they cried, "Lord, Lord, open to us," their cry was in vain. "The door was shut."

Are you ready for a New Year? Are you ready for the door to be shut on this Old Year?

Don't let the door be shut if you have not cleansed the travel stains of sin from your heart. Is someone angry with you? Go and ask him to be your friend. Do you need to ask forgivness of some friend? of God? Be prepared for a New Year.

Remove the cause of travel stains from your heart before the door is closed. A small country congregation met only once a month. Two men were leaders in the church. One wanted very much to meet each Sunday and felt they could afford a full-time pastor. The other was very stubborn and did not want to meet but once each month. When the time for the monthly meeting came the once-a-month man prayed, "Lord we have allowed lots of cob-webs to come between us and Thee since last we met. Clear away the cobwebs so that we may see thy face."

# TRAVEL STAINS (END OF YEAR)

When it came time for the every-Sunday man to pray he prayed as follows: "Lord remove the spider so we can see Thy face every Sunday."

We must remove the cause of things that have caused us to sin this past year. If it is bad companions, either win them or leave them. If it is greed, lust or plain self-interest, remove those stains from your heart.

People who have truly been washed in the blood of the lamb will be hungry for forgiveness and anxious to start afresh. Take new hope, close the door on the past and open the door on a bright new future.

### WHO CAN UNDO?

Who can undo
What time hath done? Who can win back the wind?
Beckon lost music from a broken flute?
Renew the redness of last year's rose?
Or dig the sunken sunset from the deep?
—Owen Meredith

## 27

# Stewardship

"*Bring ye all the tithes into the storehouse, that there may be meat in mine house, and prove me now herewith saith the Lord of hosts, if I will not open you the windows of heaven, and pour you out a blessing that there shall not be room enough to receive it.*"—*Malachi 3:10*

"*Will a man rob God? Yet ye have robbed me. But ye say, Wherein have we robbed thee? In tithes and offerings.*"—*Malachi 3:8*

### WILL A MAN ROB GOD? A WOMAN WILL!

I paid for my hat, I paid for my gown,
And I paid for the furs I bought down town.
But didn't have a cent I could spare
To send the gospel anywhere.

I entertained in a wonderful way,
I can "put things over" so they say.
My friends were many, they all seemed pleased,
But really I was ill at ease.

In a quiet moment I tried to see,
If I could find what was wrong with me,
A still small voice spoke in my heart
In audible tones, "Where is my part?"

## STEWARDSHIP

"Can it be true, I have no part,
No room for me within your heart?
To your friends the door is open wide.
Must your best friend stand and wait outside?"

To ease my conscience I fell on a plan
To have a little box at hand.
And when I spent a lot on myself
I'd toss a mite in the box on the shelf.

Even this did not bring relief.
The sight of it brought me to grief,
For side by side plain as could be
A mite box for Him, and a band box for me.

By this wee little box there seemed to stand
Extending to me His dear pierced hand
"I denie'd myself and was willing to give
Even my life that you might live."

I couldn't be pleased with that curious sight
So 1 determined to make it right.
I took my check book and tried to be square.
I wanted my giving to look like my prayer.

I laid on the alter one tenth of my store
And faithfully promised I'd give even more.
God opened the windows of heaven to me
There came in my soul a calm like the sea.

I said, "Oh Savior, just take my all."
And now it seems so very small.
For all that I am or hope to be
I know, O Lord I owe to Thee.
                                    —Anna Conder Heathman

A young father stood in our church one Sunday and gave a
Stewardship testimony. As he closed his message he read the
above poem and said, "The poem was written by my mother-
in-law. She has had a great influence for good on my life."

The mother-in-law lives in another city but I wrote her and
told her how very much I would like to put a copy of the
poem in this book. She replied by sending me a copy of the
poem and telling the story of how it was written. "When our

children were very young we moved to a small town in South Texas. The pastor of the little church was very young. Of course, he found out that we tithed. He asked me to write something for his small church paper. I promised to do it, but was very busy and kept putting him off. One morning he called and said he'd pick it up that evening. After the meal and the dishes were done I got my pen and paper ready but couldn't think. Then I remembered I had forgotten to ask God to help me. When I did it was very easy and was ready when he came."

Isn't that a wonderful testimony of the use God made of a Christian woman? How I hope that many thousands will hear this poem read and will be lead to tithe.

"Bless the Lord, who daily loadeth us with benefits, even the God of our salvation" (Psalm 68:19).

Many people give time to the church work; many people give money; but the blessed ones are those who give time, money and heart. We must give because we feel we love God so much we can do no less. God wants our love; the allegiance of our hearts.

One time we had car trouble on a very lonely road. We had thought to take a short cut across some ranch country and when our car stopped we were in a bad shape. At least twenty miles in any direction would have to be crossed before we could reach a filling-station.

After we were so tired from sitting and waiting two men in a truck came by. "What is wrong?" they asked.

"We are out of gas," my husband replied. "Could you help us?"

"No, we are just going to the hay barn about five miles." They drove away leaving us a deeper shade of blue than before.

After another half hour a pickup truck came by. Wearily my husband waved and asked him to stop. He stopped and offered to go to the ranch house and get some gas for us. That gas cost us a dollar a gallon but we thought it was worth every cent of the money.

# STEWARDSHIP

As Christians we have the ability to help those in need of Christ. The first men who stopped could have helped us but they did not care to be bothered. Many Christians have just that attitude about the lost world. They feel safe; have a church they like; and so, why bother with telling the story to others.

We must be good stewards. As good stewards we must give time, money, and love, so that the lost world may have the story of Jesus. God loves us. It cost Him his son. Can we truly say we love God when we drop a penny in the plate on Sunday and then go out to buy ten-cent cold drinks?

### OUR STEWARDSHIP

It is not what we earn that makes us rich
　As riches are really known,
But how honest we are as we lay our hand
　On that which we call our own.

It is not what we keep that gives us peace
　In the age when peace is rare,
But how truthful we are as we lay aside
　Our own and the Master's share.

It is not what we spend that brings us joy,
　For death can be bought with gold,
But how careful we are that nothing we buy
　Will tend to destroy our soul.

So it's not what we earn or keep or spend
　That gives us an honest glow,
But how righteous we are in the face of each
　When only ourselves will know.

　　　　　—George W. Wiseman